H. H. T

SPRING IN THE LITTLE GARDEN

The garden gate.   Within: tulips, white wistaria, forget-me-nots

THE LITTLE GARDEN SERIES

SPRING IN THE LITTLE GARDEN

BY

FRANCES EDGE McILVAINE

General Editor
MRS. FRANCIS KING

With Illustrations

BOSTON
LITTLE, BROWN, AND COMPANY
1928

THE ATLANTIC MONTHLY PRESS PUBLICATIONS
ARE PUBLISHED BY
LITTLE, BROWN, AND COMPANY
IN ASSOCIATION WITH
THE ATLANTIC MONTHLY COMPANY

To

J. W. N.

PREFACE

GLEN ISLE FARM, where is the old garden of Miss McIlvaine, dates from about 1780. It has its name partly because of a stream that wanders through the place to the east, splitting from another on the west and thus making it an "isle." The farm belongs to a family who have owned land in the valley ever since they came over from England. In its first days the present garden was not one of flowers, although the two shallow terraces on their hillside held here and there roses, bleedinghearts, and peonies. House and garden are on the south side of the valley, facing north, and on a gradual slope, a rather cold exposure. Miss McIlvaine's grandfather was a keen horticulturist, and her father was greatly interested in the garden with his daugher. Later her architect brother planned the walls, designed gates, and drew the whole together with a professional firmness for which the horticulturist owner feels deep indebtedness.

When Miss McIlvaine herself began to garden, she took the two long borders of the first and second terraces and planned to make pictures of color and form. No flowers or foliage were to be cut there, but all to remain untouched for effect. Two small squares surround big box bushes on the second terrace, one space lying to the east of the central path of the garden, one to the west, some fifty feet in each one. These squares are filled with Darwin tulips and some perennials. Other small bulbs have crept in too, and self-sown forget-me-nots, also double pink annual poppies, these followed closely for summer color by columbines and *Campanula persicifolia* and other perennials. Huge plants of sea-lavender (*statice latifolia*), *Phlox drummondi* Isabellina, a few salmon-colored phloxes, and later a few zinnias in white or pale yellow, and verbenas too, complete the list for these box-centred squares. Miss McIlvaine uses here only plants she has raised herself. She buys few, but grows most from seed or cuttings. This year there was much *Salvia farinacea* and pale yellow *Phlox drummondi*, and the planting has been good. "I keep," she writes me, "the west side of the whole garden pink and white, and the east blue and yellow, and thus it is quite easy to tone them all up or down with grays, scarlets, or lavenders. Through early summer self-sown annual larkspur feathers the whole of the borders, but is pulled out in July. I pull out always the bad colors of larkspur, and the poppies have never had any rivals to spoil their exquisite pink."

"I think," the writer adds, "everyone loves Glen Isle and says the garden has charm; it has to me because I have lived in it always, and often, even when far away, have concentrated upon the plants here and imagined changes, carrying these out later as I remembered or had the time. There are no set things in the garden or ornaments such as the gardening novice and the public seems to acquire. We have the large Italian jars, but those were bought years and years ago, before the Italian-Spanish wave. Nothing is conventional. The planting is my own, and because a plant is 'wild' it is not disqualified for trial in this garden."

Not long ago there came to me a Christmas card, a drawing of the garden of Miss McIlvaine, a long, low house with snow-covered roofs, a house "spreading its gardens to the moonlight," the high moon lighting a walled garden, a pool with snowy ice in its black waters, long, twisted festoons of wistaria stems hung in their turn with white — a most poetic picture. Above all, a picture of promise, and those who know spring at Glen Isle know that the promise is fulfilled.

From such a setting, a background rich in the work and love of gardening throughout the years, this book has sprung. All the cultivation of that old garden, as well as of the delightful people whose care and joy it has been and still is, will be found in the atmosphere of these pages. And fortunate are we who now have a book on spring gardening unlike any other here or abroad; quite unlike most American garden books thus far, in its mellow quality, born of long holding and use, and in its gayety, born of the philosophic humor of Miss McIlvaine herself.

LOUISA YEOMANS KING

CONTENTS

ILLUSTRATIONS

SPRING IN THE LITTLE GARDEN

Hortus — from the Greek χόρτος, an enclosure, as distinguished from the Latin *ager*, a field, in the open.

Hortulus — a little garden (Cicero). Cicero also used *hortulus* when he meant pleasure garden, fruit garden, kitchen garden, or vineyard.

Hortor, hortari, hortatus — the verb, though there is no connection in derivation with the noun, means, curiously enough, strongly to urge one to do a thing, to incite, exhort, instigate, encourage, cheer. All very emphatic and suitable to one starting to garden, especially that last word, to cheer.

I

BEGINNINGS, THE SPRING, SUMMER, AND AUTUMN BEFORE

I DREAMED that as I wandered by the way
Bare Winter suddenly was changed to Spring.

"BARE WINTER" need not be true of our gardens, though "bare" does describe the ground of a great part of our Middle Atlantic States at that time, too often, alas! uncarpeted by the soft, safe blanket of snow given our more northern ones. But what one can do in the bare, cold places of Pennsylvania one can do still better in the — in some ways — more fortunate snow-bound ones. Snow-bound until March and then no more, would be ideal; but it so often happens that a happy spring has come, and then arrives a late, overdue flurry of snow, or a still worse heavy one, ruining the magnolia petals, browning its on-coming buds; and another year must pass, until we see its glory of pink and white against the clear-cut gray branches.

Gardeners can never mourn for long. Too much is in the future, one lives in expectation, and if the reality attained disappoints, or if Nature fails you, do it all over again for next year, when the weather may be kinder.

No, our gardens need never be bare — with the berries of autumn still on the bushes and vines in December: crimson, gold, and purple, Berberis, Pyracantha, Callicarpa; scarlet and blue, Euonymus and Vitis; with the Christmas roses, (hellebores) opening their waxy white, pink, green, and brown-red petals from long before the holidays until February;

let us add to these the pale₁ gold flowers of all the witch-hazels, from November to March. Truly here is color for the discerning eye, and we may also have fragrance too, with the brown-yellow buds of *Meratia præcox* against a wall, some *Crocus imperati* at its feet, foretelling the still more heavenly perfume of *Viburnum carlesi* in April. We shall have the quaint *Jasminum nudiflorum* that belies its name of jasmine, having no fragrance whatever, but which will make a quiet bank glorious for weeks with its tiny gold stars, until the more brilliant forsythias take its place. On and on the days pass swiftly — snowdrops appear, and gay winter aconite; it is crocus time and *spring!*

All this in the little garden? Yes, yes, and again yes — using the word "garden" as it should be used, to mean all the ground about the house that is not used for strictly utilitarian purposes. And even there, by wall in narrow border, by vine trained on fence or trellis; for the word "garden" should also connote the word "enclosed." Long, long ago the Romans said it: *Hortus inclusus*. Long before the Romans, the Hebrews. "A garden enclosed is my sister, my spouse," says the Song of Solomon.

A low wall with a short white paling fence on top, a high wall, a chestnut woven barrier from France, a treillage, or even the hurdle fence of England now so much used about our pastures and suburban houses — any of these may be chosen for the enclosure. The hurdle fence stained a dark hue, with Euonymus planted closely and trimmed well, is good. Or in milder climates try the "fedge," that new invention so amusingly described by Clarence Elliott in the English weekly, *The Garden*. It means, he says, a light fence of palings thickly planted on each side with English ivy

(Hedera), trained and trimmed slightly. It soon forms a thick barrier, but so light it cannot be climbed over without swaying, and small, active boys are thus kept out.

Here we are reminded again of that country of gardens, England, and of her hedges that have made and guarded her gardens. That remembrance is all summed up in the rhythmic paragraphs of Amy Lowell's ringing polyphonic prose in her "Hedges of England," which must be quoted, in the hope that it may reverberate in the minds of our makers of little gardens and reveal why those "over there" hold such charm:—

Hedges of England, peppered with sloes; hedges of England, rows and rows of thorn and brier raying out from the fire where London burns with its steaming lights, throwing a glare on the sky o' nights. Hedges of England, road after road, lane after lane, and on again to the sea at the North, to the sea at the East, blackberry hedges, and man and beast plod and trot and gallop between hedges of England, clipped and clean; beech and laurel, and hornbeam.

But the plea for the enclosure has been made over and over again in the Little Garden books and in all the books on garden design. We want it here in our spring garden for weather protection and plant and bulb increase. The little garden in spring must have an abundance of the tiny bulb beauties, and they must seed and wax plentiful, now more than ever, since we cannot get them easily because of Quarantine 37.

Spring in the little garden should commence, as the Irish would say, the spring before — in any event, the autumn before. If spring be yours to plant in, procure a little magnolia tree at once, for magnolias may be moved safely only at that season. Get a *Magnolia soulangeana*, a red-pink one if possible, for under it one of the gayest pictures may be made with bulbs. Get also a *Magnolia stellata*, which will always remain a bush rather than a tree. Place these against an evergreen background if there is one. If not, make one, with a good-sized white pine or Scotch pine, the former quick, the latter slow growing, and both inexpensive. The magnolias bloom before their leaves put out and accompany the earliest bulbs, while many of the flowering cherries, the apples, and so on, do not flower until later, in tulip time.

If you have the inevitable "foundation planting" about your house, which in some suburbs seems so much overdone, be glad at least that the ground beneath may be made happy with clumps of snowdrops and many other tiny first-comers of the new year. This foundation planting and shrubbery that one may find on one's new place if one has been unfortunately forced to get a house ready-made, may contain some individually fine species bunched together with very ordinary ones by the nurseryman-planter, who finishes up these ready-made houses with his ready-made collections on the wholesale plan. Study the shrubs carefully; some may bloom early, some late; and under the early-blooming ones plant the little treasures that spring after spring may give you quantities of ever-increasing bloom that will vanish before the trials of summer begin. If the foundation planting is mostly of conifers, use these for the background needed for the little magnolias, placing them well out in front of the trees, and preferably at the side of the house, for reasons explained later. If there are any rampant growers among the shrubs, dig them out without compunction if your grounds are small, for you must have only the best. You will always find a neighbor with more space to fill, who will not listen to your well-meant warnings of suckering and spreading, — in other words, people who want quantity rather than quality, —

and to them you may generously give, though for conscience'
sake, always give them the warning too.

The snowberry (*Symphoricarpos racemosus*) is one that
spreads and has no quality. It is usually sold in all shrubbery
collections, and would soon cover a whole street of suburban
cottages, as would the other variety, the Indian or red cur-
rant (*Symphoricarpos vulgaris*). Forsythia is safe in all its
three varieties, only the drooping ones (var. *suspensa*) should
be placed on banks or walls, and the upright ones alone. And
one is usually at the mercy of the former planter here, for
forsythia is always in a shrubbery in this country, as certainly as the laurels (not our native Kalmia) are in England.

Laurel (our American kind, the Kalmia) should be in our
shrubbery, yet how rarely one sees it. Everywhere the rhododendron is being used instead, mass-planted and founda-
tion-planted, in hot sun, in poor ground, in inappropriate situations, simply because the nurserymen-landscapists can get
it in carload lots cheaply from the "collectors" who are busily
devastating the mountains, north and south. Much of it is
legitimately collected. The owner of the land is himself in
the business, and the self-sown seedlings are so plentiful and
the soil so instinct with seed that all are eventually replaced,
though the older specimens will be difficult to get as time
goes on. But it is the inappropriateness of their planting
positions that causes this protest. Kalmia grows in leaf
mould in limestone soil, which is the most usual soil around
our cities in this part of the country. Rhododendrons hate
lime, and the nurserymen-landscapists rarely take the time
or the extra cost of preparing the soil. Kalmia would grow
very much more easily if it were tried, and never puts on that
tired, worn-out look that a rhododendron assumes when the

cold weather drives the sap down from its leaves. *Kalmia latifolia* is quite difficult to get, and one does not want to start another fad and have our Pennsylvania hills robbed of their heritage more than they are at present. But we should have one or more stocky bushes of *Kalmia latifolia* — not *K. angustifolia*, the sheep laurel, which is smaller and requires moisture, as does also *K. polifolia;* and so be sure of what you are purchasing.

Euonymus japonicus is another evergreen shrub that is more preferable for backgrounds than the overdone rhododendron or the cheaper conifers, such as spruce and hemlock, that will soon outgrow their positions. The *Euonymus japonicus* is perfectly hardy in the latitude of Philadelphia. Its leaves remain as glossy as holly all winter, though sometimes it is sunburned and dies back a little on its topmost shoots. It is very handsome all the year and is easily raised from cuttings. Five or six of the Euonymus form a background for one of our rhododendron beds and are now six to eight feet high. These are about ten or twelve years old and were raised from small pieces in a sand box. Others, only three or four years old, are now in the nursery of our "truck patch," as the vegetable gardens are euphoniously called in Chester County.

It is a mistake to think all evergreens and conifers are slow growing. When one gardens, of course the years pass quickly, but it is surprising to note the long tassels the pines make each season — "plumes" would be more descriptive, as they stand up on the tips of the branches and do not hang. A box bush puts out long, pale green shoots by autumn and shows that perhaps you have bought a tree box by chance, and you should at once work for the future and take off all branches from the main stem for a space to form its trunk for posterity.

We are getting very far away from our autumn planting for our first spring in the little garden when we talk of posterity. Truly there should be a chapter on that very word, coupled to our gardens, which would show why it is so hard, so very hard, to have charm in them. With this real-estate madness sweeping over every section of every country, what can be permanent? Where will be the posterity? The bungalow is built in the middle of the lot, the garage is stuck out on one side of the rear. A collection of evergreens is spotted about or massed too close to the cellar windows. A bed of petunias runs down the front path, and four or five "For Sale" signs are sprinkled around in lieu of trees. The sale is made, and off goes the family in the flivver to start all over again in the next "development."

But sadly enough, however much we want to proselyte, with however much burning zeal we wish to teach and show the better way to garden, it is not with this sort of family we can connect the little garden. We appeal rather to those who have had the privilege of living in or near old gardens, near or with old trees, and to all who instinctively love good plants and love to watch them through all their seasons' growth.

In other words, the enchantment of the little garden in spring, as in summer and autumn and winter, depends in no small degree on the garden temperament. There must be at least one of these in the family. Sometimes they are *very* temperamental and wax furious over the scratchings and diggings of the pet cat or dog, but on the whole they are very necessary. Some people have a natural caressing love for their plants. They watch and hover over them. They plant with thought and tenderness. They have an instinctive knowledge. They know what vine will lightly cover a wall and where a lusty one is needed. They know how one will send up suckers like the trumpet vine, but that it can be kept within bounds, even developing a trunk like a dwarf tree if trained and pruned in time. All this knowing how has come bit by bit since childhood, if there has been an observing eye. Others must learn by trial and error, as the psychologists say. No friend can warn, no book direct; they will have it thus and so; failure simply makes them more determined. They will dig it from there and place it here, they say, and so they have the hope and thrill of expectation all over again. This is the vital pleasure of their sort of gardening. We need of course several kinds of garden temperament, but they should all be of the inquiring variety. A surprising number of gardening people are not inquiring, and never know their plants all the way through from cellar to attic, one might say, from root beginning to seed finishing. Some never know, for instance, how the crocus, long after its flowers have vanished, sends up a mysterious white-covered cone, one of the most interesting of seed packets. The seeds have done a great part of their ripening below ground, so when they appear it is nearly time to gather them. All species of crocus, save two, do this.[1] The true handmaid of Nature sows these seeds, and in the third or fourth year they will bloom. Where is the family that will remain in one home at least four years? And when we read in Mr. Bowles's book on the Crocus[2] that he waited for thirty years before he got a white seedling of one species to reward his patience, we wonder if there exists any American family who will attain either this patience or this permanency.

[1] *C. caspius* and *C. korolkowii* do not push their seed capsules above the surface of the soil.

[2] *A Handbook on Crocus and Colchicum for Gardeners*, by E. A. Bowles, M.A.

II

PICTURES WITH BULBS

I WALK down the garden paths,
And all the daffodils
Are blooming and the bright blue squills.
"Patterns," AMY LOWELL

THE little garden has one advantage over the big one: it is apt to be — nay, has to be — near, close up to the house, and in spring this is an inestimable boon. For often the only good weather we have in spring is in our memories of other years. Then that snow did not come so late or quite so cruelly. Then the winds were not so high or so constant, and there were days when we worked out of doors for hours. Whereas, *this* year, just look at the rain! And we gaze disconsolately out of the window. But if we have planned wisely, our view out of that window and every other window will give us interest. For we shall see our dream pictures of color and form coming true with the days' progress, even though the sun may not shine, and the winds may blow too strongly for us to be out.

Let us begin to create the first picture, which is built about the magnolia tree spoken of before. It should be within sight of a room that is much used in daytime; the dining room is perhaps the only one in these modern days that sees the family very often. And let us hope you can commence, as has been said, the autumn before, having planted the magnolia the spring of that year. Under it you are going to make a fairy ring — not a true circle, for no fairy would like anything so set and formal, but a wide irregular band of gradually unfurling blossom from the tiny first arrivals of spring. For the diagram, take the children's big jumping rope, laid on the ground in long, undulating curves. You have already bought, begged, or borrowed as many of the following bulbs as possible: snowdrops, *Scilla sibirica*, winter aconite, glory-of-the-snow, grape hyacinths, crocus, *Scilla bifolia*, and even a few dwarf narcissi such as W. P. Milner or minimus, and fritillaries — in fact, any small, any early species. For most of these you will have to pay five dollars a hundred where you used to pay five shillings, but some you can buy from old gardens if you happen to see them in time. These, dug and planted in shallow boxes in spring when you see them in bloom, and ripened off, can be added in autumn to the other ingredients for the fairy ring. If you won't beg you can always borrow — which means, in the gardener's dictionary, that you repay with anything (in reason) that the borrowed-from person wants in return, as the season waxes and wanes. One takes into consideration the person's gardening accuracy as to value. Do not give, for instance, the rare Eremurus in exchange for Verbascum; though both give the same effect, their values are quite different. Eremurus for Camassia would be fairer.

But to go back to your bulbs, the very earliest are the snowdrops. John Weathers, in his Bulb book, lists thirteen varieties, so if you buy everything under Galanthus from several dealers, you may get some of the rarer snowdrops that were plentiful in all English and Dutch catalogues before the war. In old gardens in the Southern States, Leucojums are called snowdrops; these were brought over probably by the early English colonists. *Leucojum vernum* does so well,

gives so many flowers, and is so much more showy than the
Galanthus that it might give more satisfaction than the true
snowdrop, though no flower of early spring has the startling
whiteness of *Galanthus Elwesi Poculi*. Even one solitary
bloom will light up a bare corner surprisingly, and seems to
stand with gracious reserve and dignity. The small ones —
G. nivalis — increase very quickly and grow in the poorest
soil, so we can have plenty of these in a few years, from their
own seed.

Of *Scilla sibirica*, one hundred will not look very much the
first year, but they seed enormously, and if you have a friend
with an old garden you may gather seeds and the tiny bulb-
lets that are as thick as peas on the ground and just beneath
it in any large planting. The Eranthis (winter aconite) is
the gayest early comer, with its brilliant yellow face and Eliz-
abethan ruff of green. As this is a modern garden, we should
have only the best for our little space, so choose the new
hybrid made by Mr. Van Tubergen and called for him. It
is far larger and brighter, also more expensive, but having
bought but ten for our garden, it was encouraging to find
they made a brave show of golden yellow, being so much
larger than the old kinds. This hybrid, however, is sterile,
while the others seed freely and spread more quickly. There
are only three other varieties of Eranthis besides this new hybrid; they are *E. cilicia*, *hyemalis*, and *sibirica*. You may of
course try all, as the rightly curious gardener should. The
Eranthis "bulb" is really a rootstock or tuber, like the
anemones, and it is a constant marvel how life can come out of
such a dried-up, hard brown morsel.

The glory-of-the-snow (Chionodoxa) is exquisite — pale
china blue and bright sky-color, also a pure white variety

which should be made to intermarry with the others. It is twice as costly, so you need not get so many. Then the scillas — the catalogues list six or seven varieties under the species *S. campanulata* and *S. nutans*, but for this place you only want *S. sibirica* — and *S. bifolia* if you can get it. The first two bloom in May and you wish the very earliest here as the fairy ring must appear from the ground by magic in the bleak March days.

The strength of the planting will lie with the crocus; we must have the Scotch one, which did not come from Scotland at all but probably from Spain, — it is *C. biflorus*, — also many *C. Tomasinianus*, a tiny early blue and blue-and-white, and the golden ones which send up so many flowers from one corm that even fifty will go a very long way; and the lavender-and-white striped ones that always suggest Easter, and Easter is apt to come just when the crocuses are doing their best. No one really knows the crocus until he has seen them in masses, increasing from year to year as they will do under our trees and in the open soil of flower beds. They are too often put in grass, their tops mown off before they ripen, and so soon dwindle away.

It is quite a laborious proceeding to plant a fairy ring. To return to the children's jumping rope, laid out on the ground in curves and bays — one must do this planting one's self; no one else will take the trouble. But if the ground is hard and unyielding, a digger can be gotten to turn out a trench, following the line, taking out about half a foot of earth. Then, equipped with a bucket of sand, another of peat mull, — or peat moss, that valuable new ingredient, — also a little can of powdered sulphur to keep field mice away and to show yourself next year, if you stir the soil, that bulbs are planted here — down on your knees you may go, your bulbs all out of their bags and coco-shell wrappings on trays, separate trays, on the grass. If you have many of the yellow crocus, it is well to put these all around the ring first, about a foot apart in groups of twos or threes — this will make a bit of sun for surety. Most of these little bulbs need only two or three inches of soil above them, but it is best to have the half-foot taken out of the trench, and mix some bone meal with it, removing stones, and putting back a little earth mixed with peat mull and an inch or less of sand under each hill.

Gather, then, the other bulbs by twos and threes; set them on their cushion of sand, dash the sulphur on both sides of the trench, and fill in gently with the soil mixed with peat. Oh, but you will be weary and your knees will ache, yet you will never think of this when March and April come! The warm October sun is caressing you while you toil, and apples and other autumn plenty are at hand to refresh you. After the tiny ones are all underground, and the top is patted firmly and outlined with more sulphur, so memory will not fail you that your work there is done and so the hired man may be warned off, you must wait until a hard freeze comes before covering lightly with salt hay or more peat moss. This keeps the cruel cracks of frost from wrenching the ground and throwing the bulbs out. So, all is done, and you await the white blanket of snow and the slow months of winter. Then in March and April, as the buds swell and winds and sun are kind, behold the little magnolia tree standing proudly, spreading its great pink-and-white blooms, while beneath appears your fairy ring, all gold and white and blue. Thus it will be an unending delight each successive year. And its memory should reconcile the gardener to keeping the grass there uncut until the bulbs all ripen and the seeds mature and fall. It will look fringe-like and unkempt for a time, but if the eye is trained to it, it appears just as beautiful as the shorn lawn and trim borders that can be at the other side of the house.

Another picture may be made, to view from the kitchen door or window if the kitchen is at the back of the house where all well-behaved ones used to be. As automobiles and trucks increase in number, making more dust and noise on our streets, many architects are putting the rear of the house at the entrance door — kitchen, garage, and all. The living rooms then face the quiet inner sanctuary of the remaining ground, as they should. But this can only be done when all the surrounding houses do the same, so it waits the town-planning of the future, which will be the Little Garden's paradise,

To return to things as they are, we shall hope to find a brick pavement across the back. It will be more apt to be a cement one, but we can make a coping or edge of brick on end, and so get a touch of the warm reddish-pink color contrasting with the brown soil of the strip of border which must be dug on either side. Here is the place to put the "daffodils and the bright blue squills." And the hyacinths, the heavenly scented hyacinths, how perfect they are, giving out their fragrance on the frail spring air! They never look better than when planted in a narrow, confined space such as this. It gives the same gayety that a mass of tulips gives, but the delicious odor adds a more joyous note. The daffodils and squills (*Scilla sibirica*) may be left in the bed many years, and so may the hyacinths, but in small formal beds such as these it is better to get fine varieties of bulbs, and dig, dry, and store for the summer. The gardener's trowel will otherwise strike and slice them when bedding plants are put in. All bulbs are now too costly to waste where such accidents may occur.

There is a great pleasure in digging, drying off, and storing bulbs if one gets interested in doing it skillfully, but it takes time, and some people will prefer bridge or country-clubbing. No hired man can do it carefully enough; varieties will get mixed and labels lost. So unless one plans to do it one's self, jot down another expense item and buy new bulbs every year. Or else give up this picture entirely and do the following one instead, which is permanent and easy. This effect takes place at the very entrance door of my home, and very early, even in March, it begins. It is adapted to many homes, I think, even to those whose owners go away for most of the summer, for it presents a sober dark green surface all the year, except during the spring. There is a bit of brightness again in autumn, when colchicums, autumn crocus, and sternbergia bloom.

On each side of the entrance door, down the path to the gate, or to the drive, even if there is only a narrow bit of ground by the terrace, plan a space as wide as you can in proportion to the house and door. Gather together again all the minor bulbs you can, as you did for the fairy ring. Get also many small tufts of periwinkle (*Vinca minor*) from anyone who has banks of it, or from the nurseryman specializing in ground-covering plants. Do not get Pachysandra, as its roots are too coarse and voracious. Dig up the soil well; it does not have to be deeply dug, and small stones do not matter, but rather add to its texture. Plant more crocus than anything else; in drifts and groups they will seed

together after a while. On the outer edges put the scillas and
chionodoxas. The snowdrops can go in the "worst" places,
under the eaves or near the steps, for they persist anywhere.
If there is shade to come from trees leafing out later, hepaticas, a bloodroot or two, trilliums, and other native things
may be used. Spaces may be left and marked the first year
for the summer-planted ones for autumn bloom, the colchicums, autumn crocus, sternbergias, and hellebores, which
must be set in July and August. These are all strong and
permanent occupants. The colchicums are large bulbs, the
Crocus speciosus a never-failing variety, and the sternbergias
will recall April again with their golden-yellow daffodil-like
flowers. The hellebores will open a new field of delight in
autumn and winter when their name, "Christmas roses,"
becomes a reality. The leaves of these plants in spring will
mingle with the green of the periwinkle. Those of the colchicum are rather obtrusive, but they soon lay themselves
down to ripen and the arching stems of the vinca will hide
them. It is marvelous how the crocus and other small creatures will increase, and how the periwinkle will spread until
the whole space is first starred white with snowdrops, gleam-
ing with crocus, purple, white, and gold, then blue with scilla
and chionodoxa, dainty with hepatica and bloodroot, and
at last green and lustrous with the kindly covering vinca and
its gray-blue, wide-open flowers. The first year or two one
must pull out grass and weeds, and always there will be the
need for cutting away the periwinkle roots where they seem
to be too heavy over the bulbs, but they make a very happy
combination. *Sedum acre* and *Sedum sexangulare* may be
used where the periwinkle does not take hold readily.

We all have pictures in our mind's eye of meadows of

daffodils. "Naturalizing in orchards" is a favorite phrase of garden writers. Where there is plenty of space this is all very well, but one dislikes to see groups under a few trees with the grass all cut away neatly around them as if they had just had their hair shingled. I know one small place where the daffodils dance beneath the trees, waving in long grass as they should, and only paths are cut through where one strolls to enjoy; this is much more charming than patch-planting, shorn around by the scissors. If the grounds are large enough to have a small vegetable plot, put the better and newer daffodils there. All daffodils, we know, are narcissi, but not all narcissi are daffodils; these mean to us only the yellow, ranging from the sweet-scented jonquil to the bicolor trumpet. The rarer ones, both yellow and white, short-cupped and long-cupped, long-trumpet and short-trumpet, should go in rows, carefully marked with their names, to increase, and for cutting, and even for seed if one wants the interest of hybridizing. A drawing of this planting should be made at once and filed away for reference at blooming time. I call these diagrams "maps," and have a most curious lot of them. If illuminated in color rather than by experience, they would give a vivid picture of success and failure.

Some years ago, when this extreme quarantine was threatened, a wise friend urged me to get a few, even a very few each, of the high-priced, high-bred narcissi that were being displayed at all the British shows, raised by Mrs. Backhouse, the Rev. Joseph Jacob, and other remarkable English, Scotch, and Irish hybridists. I got a few, — alas, a very few, — and this same wise friend sent me others for several years. Now how I wish I had put in more! for their increase is certain and their beauty astounding; and their texture is so strong, each flower lasts three times as long as the older sorts, when left on the stem or when cut for the house.

As for pictures with narcissi, they are more satisfying as single flowers to study and marvel over. Their shape and structure are so wonderful it raises one's spirit to contemplate them. Every form, every variety seems a perfect creation: the cup, edged scarlet, some of the newest ones being entirely scarlet; the long, dome-like, fluted trumpet of pale primrose or deepest yellow; the wide flare of the perianth (why should it be so pure white in the bicolors, so richly golden in the selfs?); the fragrance, so different in the poeticus from the Leedsi and Barri — every point is one to rejoice over and to reverence. But if one only wishes the daffodil as a splash of color out of doors, plant Golden Spur for early bloom and Emperor or Empress for late, in large groups of fifty or more at the ends of the flower borders or in spaces in the shrub plantings.

We have not yet arrived at the tulip season, and this bulb is one that can never exhaust all the possibilities of picture arrangement. From the early tulip to the Cottage varieties, through the Darwins, the Breeders, and the Parrots to the Bybloems and Bizarres, there will not be a space left nor room to make collections of any. So for the tulips, if there is to be a space of ground called "the garden" around the house, apart from the whole plot being called so, let it be formal and box-edged. In these mathematical triangles and curves put the tulips. Nothing will set them off so well as the dark green box leaves. But resign yourself to doing it every year afresh, so make the parterres small.

One other picture the practical housewife home maker will achieve, if ever Blue Monday's produce has to mar her precincts. She will have a cement socket inserted in the grass plot where the sun shines best, and there erect a pole holding one of those great spiked-wheel affairs that turn in the wind. This, when hung with the bright garments of the children, with jumpers and rompers of orange, scarlet, and blue, will look like some huge gay flower as the spring gale whirls it about, drying them swiftly. After which the pole can come down and be laid away until the next week's blossoming.

III

NATIVE MATERIAL VERSUS FOREIGN

Happy the man, whose wish and care
A few paternal acres bound,
Content to breathe his native air
In his own ground.

ALEXANDER POPE

WE always want most that which we cannot easily have —
in gardens as in everything else. So now that the quarantine
on bulbs has commenced in earnest, barring out the narcissi
entirely, and its further threat against the "minor bulbs"
has automatically caused the disillusioned foreign growers
to raise the prices on them, many have become practically
out of the question for mass planting. We now hear rumors
of the probable exclusion of all crocuses, hyacinths, tulips,
and every other bulb in the near future, so we must turn
sternly away from all these traditional joys, and seek out our
native plants for spring. They are still somewhat hard to get
in quantity commercially, and many are not yet easily grown,
because we have not so far applied ourselves diligently to
learn their needs.

Our own are, in many ways, just as beautiful as the traditional and storied flowers. One is convinced that all they
need is an aureole of romance or anecdote written about them
to make them familiar to our gardening world. Some of the
loveliest thrills of spring come from our own American plants
— thrills that an Englishman takes infinite pains to plan
for, to import for. One remembers, in an English garden
book, the writer saying he longed to see a North American
wood in spring with its masses of *Sanguinaria canadensis*

shining white amid the green. This rhapsody caused a gentle smile, for we know, as a matter of fact, our *Sanguinaria canadensis* (bloodroot) never in its native haunts is very showy. Its white petals usually stand out from a background of sere brown forest leaves that do not set them off very gayly. But, planted in one's garden in a setting of periwinkle (myrtle, *Vinca minor*), it is really startling in beauty, and its own handsome leaves, coming a bit later, are interesting and lasting.

Then consider the *Mertensia virginica*, the bluebell of the Brandywine, as it is called up and down that historic stream near my home in Pennsylvania, the loveliest of flowers, with its sky blue bells, tipped pink to an opalescent hue. If tradition and poetry clustered about Mertensia one half as much as around many English flowers, it would be loved and planted and propagated everywhere. But because its simple habits are not studied, and because it has not this halo of garden lore, it remained unheralded until one of the large firms of the country, in the new mad rush for advertising and boosting stock, sent a colored plate of it broadcast, advocating its planting — at a high price — in clumps. Soon it will come into general use, with the tragic result, no doubt, of its disappearing eventually from its old haunts, due to the zeal of collectors, who will resell to the big nurserymen, who now fill the heavy pages of our gardening journals with their heavier and more expensive advertisements of "new and rare" plants.

The Mertensia, placed in association with our *Trillium grandiflorum*, makes a most enchanting combination. Neither is very particular as to soil, and both disappear obligingly after blooming and ripening their seed, so a corner may easily

be given to them under a group of deep-rooting shrubs or
beneath a tree. With me they grow along the banks of a
stream which is very often dry in summer, and a light woodland grass grows over their graves. But they come back
every spring and are now seeding around near by. Plant
both, of course, in autumn, but if transplanting, do it as the
leaves commence to yellow, for after that, when they disappear, you won't find them at all, and they say Mertensia is
so sensitive she will not bloom the next year if you acciden-
tally strike her with a trowel when digging about. As for
myself, I have not found this true. There are several other
Mertensias, native to the West, one with yellow bells that
sounds attractive.

The dogtooth violet (*Erythronium americanum*) is another
genus of our very own — at least, of its eighteen species all
but one, the old *E. dens-canis* of Europe, are natives of North
America. Our Eastern yellow ones, called trout lilies in New
England, are lovely enough, but the California and Oregon
varieties are beautiful too, and quite exotic-looking in white,
lavender, and rose. All grow easily in a gritty soil well en-
riched with leaf mould. We should now say peat moss or
mull instead of leaf mould; as it is so very easy and cheap to
buy, it should supersede the difficult scraping and doubtful
ethics of digging in our neighbor's woods, trying to get a little
bagful of the pesky stuff, all instinct with weed seeds anyway.
Dogtooth violets bloom very early and may go under the
kalmia or rhododendron bushes.

Our wild geranium (*Geranium maculatum*) or cranesbill is
very easy and a good increaser. If one finds or buys a white
variety, it soon forms a beautiful mound of snowy bloom that
is lovely with some of the violets of the roadside. Unfragrant

though they are, our wild violets have such wonderful color and profuse bloom that one is tempted to bring into the garden some especially good forms, even though they must be uprooted and thrown out soon after flowering for fear of their thousands of progeny lurking in their seed packets hiding so unobtrusively just above ground — those white globules of seed that burst silently below their canopy of rounded green leaves, scattering millions of little violets-to-be where they are not wanted.

Our most precious American plant and our earliest is the arbutus, the mayflower of New England (*Epigæa repens*). No longer is it so difficult to grow since the experiments of our Department of Agriculture and Dr. Wherry have given us the secret of acid soil and of making the environment suit the plant. When our civilization becomes as old as that of the Chinese, it may be that we can get the exquisite enjoyment they do from fragrance and beauty in plants. It is said that a Chinese scholar can contemplate a stalk of feathery grass upon his desk for hours with rapture, and a certain variety of quince is grown merely for its fragrant fruit, which is used to perfume their rooms. We, if we could but grow our arbutus in pots as they do in the experimental greenhouses in Washington, D. C., could get exquisite pleasure from its fragrance and the chaste, frosty beauty of its flowers. There is no perfume quite like it; and what memories does it not evoke! It would be so easy, if we were a bit more skillful, to arrange pots of it to gladden the first spring days. If our commercial florists would do this, how much better would it be to purchase these as gifts for the shut-in or invalid, instead of the tightly wadded bunches of the collectors, who are swiftly exterminating it.

The yellow ladyslipper (*Cypripedium pubescens*) is not a difficult plant, though its relative, *C. hirsutum*, is harder for ordinary gardens, as it needs constantly moist soil. And remember that when planting the ladyslipper, — which must be bought from a dealer, as it will be a better plant with its own ball of roots, — we should plant a clump of maidenhair fern (*Adiantum pedatum*) by it to shade it partially and also to mark its home, for it disappears after blooming, while the fern continues to grow all summer if in partial shade and sometimes watered. One friend of mine has been very successful with native plants from her adjoining wood, placed right at the base of the house wall on its north side. Narrow beds were left between the wall and the wide flagged terrace, dug out deeply and filled with leaf soil, this time from the woods, as they were her own! Here all ferns, bulbs native and imported, the wintergreen, and the arbutus have made themselves at home, but they have been watered and made welcome by their faithful owner. I am mentioning only the American plants that we have grown for early spring in my own experience. There are hosts of others. Each section of the country should know and grow its own, and by experimenting and propagating, build up a technique, as Mr. Stephen Hamblin of the Harvard Botanic Garden desires. Then if we also build up — as we mentioned before — a tradition, an aureole of legend or romance about them, generations to come will cherish them as our cousins the English love their primrose and their hawthorn. For it is very true that sentiment and memory play a large part in our love for familiar objects. With which bit of sermonizing let us continue to describe a few more beauties.

Hepatica triloba (liverwort) we are told to buy, as it is

rapidly being exterminated. This and its southern and west-
ern relative, *H. acutiloba*, can be easily secured from dealers
and they succeed almost anywhere. Their furry collars surrounding their sky blue, pale pink, and white faces are even
more appealing than the Eranthis (winter aconite), with its
bright yellow face and green fringed ruff, that we must now
forego under the quarantine. Once, in the West, I saw a garden whose woodland paths were edged as thickly with
hepaticas as we would use wild violets or gray-leaved pinks.
Exclaiming with pleasure, but thinking the simultaneous
thought of how costly it must have been to buy from the
dealer, — or how wrong from a conservationist's point of
view to collect from the wild,— we were told that all we saw
had been rescued from a real-estate development in the neigh-
borhood. The seeing eye had noted and in the nick of time
rescued all the dear little furry-hooded plants from the voracious steam shovel and the workmen's spades.

Jack-in-the-pulpit (*Arisæma triphyllum*) and Mayapple
(*Podophyllum peltatum*) we must have — one plant of the
Jack, he looks more dignified thus, and one umbrella or two
of the Mayapple, which must not be allowed to spread. The
children love to play with them and can be taught to leave
them on their stalks. Their game will go quite as well as
pulling up bunches in the woods to throw away in half an
hour. Spring beauties (*Claytonia virginica*) will sow themselves, but blue-eyed-grass or *Sisyrinchium angustifolium*
(such a name!) and Quaker ladies (*Houstonia cærulea*) are
harder to establish, in my experience; but then I expect to
gain a great deal more experience, thanks, we may one day
say, to the Federal Horticultural Board's arbitrary quarantine and the spur of necessity.

With the daffodils bought before the quarantine or the few
and expensive ones bought afterward, plant of course the
lovely pale blue *Phlox divaricata*, that elusive phlox that we
think we shall have in masses this spring as we had it last
year; we cannot understand why it disappears. Another case
of the need for knowing a plant from root to seed. Over
and over again I have grown it and given it away, only to be
told in a year or so, "My dear, you know that phlox — that
lovely blue one, I never can remember the name? Oh, yes,
divaricata; well, my dear, it has simply vanished; may I
have some more? Well, I *would* rather have it in the fall, but
perhaps I had better take it now." And one may wager an
extra clump of daffodils they will *not* have it by fall, and
spring will find them as mystified as before. Why? Because
Phlox divaricata in bloom does not look one bit like itself
when seeding in autumn. In bloom it is heavenly, a cloud of
soft gray-blue on slender, almost leafless stalks; seeding,
these stalks and few leaves look dusty and unattractive. They
are cut off by the tidy gardener, and, ten to one, are weeded
up by the handy man as he cleans the front of the border.
Safer, far safer, to have your clumps far back in the bed and
always some in a reserve place to propagate from. After
blooming, pull the plant apart; sometimes it has run along
the ground and its wiry black stem will have roots at inter-
vals along the joints. Separate these and put all in a row,
water a little, and by autumn there will be a nice lot of dark
green, shiny-leaved, woodland-looking plants, that appear
very different from the gray-green dusty ones you set out
in June after the lovely blue cloud of flowers had disappeared.
These you can plant where you know you need them: where
some yellow primroses are, where the daffodils are coming,

The garden before the hedges grew.   Tulips, Phlox divaricata, and Primula acaulis

and where the pale pink Cottage tulips appear; for they bloom a long time and will be with the late daffodils as well as the early and late Cottage tulips, though not with the Darwins and Breeders.

We have a number of small trees and shrubs native to our own land, that are especially beautiful with their spring bloom. Earliest of all comes the shadbush (*Amelanchier canadensis*), whose white flowers vanish almost as soon as they appear, but look charming planted near the redbud (*Cercis canadensis*). All the wild cherries, especially the bird cherries (*Prunus pennsylvanica*) and the hawthorns, of which there are two hundred native species, are good. If they are raised from seed, which is easily done, a number of lovely forms result, giving us clouds of white flowers in May and deep scarlet-red fruit in October. But when we say "hawthorn" we are back in English tradition again, so use the word "Cratægus" unless you plant the Washington thorn (*Cratægus phaenopyrum* or *C. cordata* of dealers), which gives this one a patriotic tinge. The cratægus has style, a sturdy, finished look. One often sees it across a bare meadow, near a stream, and wonders what that fascinating bush is. It looks well alone or in groups, would never need the pruning shears, and holds its leaves and berries well into the winter. Then there are the American crabs (*Pyrus coronaria*) and the dogwoods (*Cornus florida*), but most lovely and unusual of all are the silverbell tree (Halesia) and the fringetree (*Chionanthus retusa*). This last adds enchanting fragrance to its other charms. There is a Chinese variety, said to have longer filaments, as its blossoms may be called. They are greenish white and hang in clusters several inches long. I have the Chinese variety, which, though some seven years old, has not yet bloomed. Our native one, however, has been a source of pleasure for years. The silverbell (Halesia) is also unusual, and one should plant bulbs beneath, getting lovely effects from contrasts of color, for its bells are snow white, and scarlet, yellow, or pink tulips would make good foils for it. Both these trees will turn into shrubby bushes if watch is not kept over them when young; and as they establish themselves much better when planted in their youth, keep an eye on their main trunk-to-be.

One's pride in one's own native plants and trees is stirred by reading the Life of Peter Collinson and his letters to John Bartram, our first botanist and horticulturist. With what eagerness did the old English Quaker in London write for seeds and plants, and how enthusiastic he and his friends, among them the young Lord Petrie, became over the boxes sent them from Pennsylvania! The talented Lord Petrie came to an untimely death, but his plants survived, among them the tulip poplar, which they all regarded, and rightly, as a most wonderful acquisition. They kept the first one sent over in a pot, putting it into the orangery each winter, fearing it would not survive out of doors. But one winter they forgot it, and behold, it grew much better and soon shot into a tall tree. One can imagine seeing or hearing of the flower of the Liriodendron; one might well think it was an exotic species, and fear to trust the only plant in the country to the rigors of winter, which, as it happened, were far less severe in England than in its own land.

IV

APARTMENT–HOUSE PLANTINGS FOR
SMALL BORDERS

An English artist, Frank Miles, for whom a charming daffodil is named, coined this title, "apartment-house plantings." He said, "Why should we restrict our gardens to one layer of planting — we ourselves live on many floors in our houses; many of us must live on but one of many floors in our apartment houses; why not arrange our flower borders on the same plan?" Put first the bulbs that can grow from great depth. Some of the lilies, we know, are not happy unless they are eight or even twelve inches below the surface. Do not forget the sand they like to sit on, or even the flat cool stone that Mr. E. H. Wilson of the Arnold Arboretum says is often found just touching their base in their native haunts. Some tulips do well at seven or eight inches and do not seem to be so prolific of increase at this depth. Here also should be put *Amaryllis halli* for bloom in late summer. Then come hyacinths. Hyacinths are not used enough in American gardens. They seem to be relegated to park bedding arrangements; yet what is more delicious than their perfume on spring evenings? They are very permanent, and by getting fifty or even twenty-five of the Dutch third size, or miniature, as they are called by the trade, one may expect them to appear for years. The single are the best for this purpose, and gradually the groups with the added increasing smaller spikes of bloom will give many for cutting. Of course they are not at all like the great fat columns of the named varieties, such as the magnificent Lord Derby, but resemble the graceful Romans which many find more attractive.

Higher now we go to our next level of planting for the narcissus tribe, though some of these may go six or even seven inches down. But one follows the rule of once-and-a-half the depth of the bulb, using this varying measurement for the amount of earth to place on top of it. The deeper-rooting perennials must go between these bulb groups, so one should have a sketched-out plan and attempt this all in one's first October-made border. Mark the deepest spots to be left for the lilies that will not be shipped you until December, such as the auratums, speciosums, and so on. Here we shall insert the usual remark when lilies are the subject of conversation, and which is now almost a platitude: "All excepting the Madonna (*lilium candidum*), which should be in the ground by September,"—though it is rarely shipped by then, — and is planted but two or three inches below the surface, and the inevitable *Delphinium belladonna* with it, though I prefer to make other combinations, such as white foxgloves or blue-and-white *Campanula persicifolia*, and the foliage of the thalictrums.

The roots of perennials are very interesting studies, and the apartment-house borders must take cognizance of them. The gardener must have a mental sketch of the root habits of each plant, being careful that a long, fleshy tuber does not strike an up-coming tulip spear, or that the spongy mass of thalictrum roots is not directly above the heavy cone-shaped bulbs of the camassias.

One of the most satisfactory borders that I have runs somewhat like this: Along the front are old clumps of daffodils and an occasional hyacinth group; farther back, arrangements of from ten to twelve Darwin tulips. On top of the daffodils are such light-rooting plants as *Stachys lanata*, for its gray velvety leaves, *Phlox divaricata*, and *Pulmonaria*, for their quantities of early blue bloom. Back of this are large plants of lemon lily (*Hemerocallis flava*) and *Astilbe japonica*, the tulips between. Sometimes the Hemerocallis encroaches over the tulips, but it can always be pulled out when the tulips show, as the lily has small fleshy tubers that come away easily from the clump and may be planted at once elsewhere. The *Astilbe japonica* is a good stocky white one, bearing its creamy plumes in late July; it does not conflict in color with anything and its leaves are lovely as they unfold, fernlike, in early spring. A band of crocus about a foot wide is back of this. It makes the border very gay in late March and April, and the corms increase so by seeding in the open soil that an occasional digging up by mistake in summer does not matter. Gypsophila, only the double variety or the new one, Bristol Fairy, must be put in carefully here and there. Its roots go down very deeply in a carrotlike formation; it does not take up any space underneath, though a great deal above, and it must not be permitted to send its spiky root down for example, on top of one's most precious *hansoni* lily. *Thalictrum flavum* and *T. dioicum* are set along the back for their foliage, and this genus takes up a great deal of room both up and down, going and coming. One must remember the Hemerocallis, as said above, will spread in time, as will also *Iris germanica*, but all will do well for a few years.

There are a great many associations of bulbs and perennials that may be made like this in apartment-house borders, but there is always the danger of the disappearance of an entire group as well as the unexpected delight of the increase of another. Also one must be wary of an arrangement read about or told one, that has been successful in another section of our country. The Nankeen lily (*L. testaceum*) was said to be charming rising up through the mist of a flowering gypsophila. In my Pennsylvania garden the lily came up, bloomed, and passed on, before the gypsophila commenced its white haze of tiny flowers.

In a long border of peonies placed about three feet apart, orange and red Breeder tulips look especially well, as the young shoots of the peonies show bronze and red in harmony. Such a border, full of golden crocus, set with yellow pansies or with violas, Cheiranthus (the Siberian wallflower), and Erysimum that is very like it, from a kindly wintering cold-frame, will be a brilliant joy for weeks. If the peonies are chosen in white and cream only, oriental poppies in the type, the scarlet, which is more permanent than the lovely salmon and white hybrids, may alternate with them, but this takes us up to June, so we must abdicate to summer, though the temptation to indicate this orange-red border all the way to autumn is a strong one.

It is much safer and more satisfactory for cutting and other purposes to put the narcissi in rows to themselves, as we have said elsewhere. One may use the space all season too, for as their leaves ripen they may be braided together and tucked out of sight, if one does not wish to lift them that year. Light-rooting annuals such as asters or cosmos may be dibbled in between from small pots. Both these are indispensable for cutting later, and if put in early from pots will have plenty of roots to go ahead on, without danger to the narcissi bulbs beneath.

In the little garden it is hard to have a cutting space as well as a picture space, but as one of our Little Garden Series designates a "little" garden as from fifty to one hundred feet, or from three to five acres, one can but pick and choose. There are two kinds of flower lovers. One loves to cut the flowers and to fill bowls and vases; she cuts and cuts, regardless of length of stem or number of buds; she cuts and cuts, and leaves a total absence of bloom behind her. The other snips and snips, but never a flower for bowl or vase does she have at the end of her journey around the garden. Each snip has taken off an unwieldy branch or removed a dead flower or an unwanted seed pod. Yet at the rose bed this other does pause, and cuts roses for the house, treating the bush with care for future bloom, taking not too long a stem, cutting just above a leaf, allowing for the new flower-bearing stalk to spring from the joint. For this garden artist the picture is the thing. There stand the tulips with certain foliage or wall as background; what reason to cut these for one day's brief glory in the overheated house? There must be flowers in the house also, but to the picture gardener often comes the thought: "If I cannot have both, let me leave the dear creatures to live their lives out on their own stems and roots. I will have this Japanese shell flower or that Chinese tree of porcelain to contemplate indoors."

V

SPECIALTIES FOR SPRING

For love we Earth, then serve we all;
Her mystic secret then is ours.
"A Reading of Earth," George Meredith

I have spoken at some length of many of the early comers, as we name these brave flowers, the winter aconite (Eranthis) the snowdrop (Galanthus), and the crocus. There are many others as easy to grow, yet rarely seen. Some of these are old companions of mine, so I feel well qualified to tell of them and perhaps bring them into other gardens. Alphabetically the list should commence with *Adonis amurensis* or *A. vernalis.* I thought I had the former, but suspect it is the latter since reading Darnell, whose *Winter Blossoms from an Outdoor Garden* has struck many an answering chord in me. *A. amurensis* is, he says, native to Japan, and comes in many colors, from yellow to rose, purple, and scarlet, whereas *A. vernalis* is only yellow and white. Mine has a cheerful yellow double flower, with an accompaniment of finely cut fernlike leaves, and it has a never-failing habit of appearing very early in April and disappearing by May. It is dependable, has a long life, and does not spread, an herbaceous perennial from nine to eighteen inches high, listed in many catalogues as procurable in this country.

Camassias come next, though taking them alphabetically plays havoc with their blooming schedule, for camassias bloom in May just ahead of the Darwin tulips. They are a group of bulbous plants from our own Northwest and Canada,

Camassia Cusickii. A bulb from northwest America, a stately stalk of pale blue

but, like many others, went across to Europe to be hybridized into new and improved forms. Such a one is the variety of the photograph, *Camassia cusicki*, pale blue with yellow stamens. It always causes admiring remarks, and the usual query is, "Where *did* you get it? Where can I get it now, since the quarantine?" The native ones may be gotten from California — possibly Oregon — nurseries, and are quite good. They are usually dark blue; the varieties *C. leichtlini* and *alba* are taller, with flowers wider apart than the *cusicki*. The bulbs are large and cone-shaped, somewhat like a carrot or a parsnip upside down; they are extremely hardy and good increasers. The Indians called them "quamash" and ate them as we do potatoes. Here is a good field for hybridizers. The seed takes two years to germinate.

Chimonanthus fragrans is a brown-yellow flowering shrub that blooms from November to March if it likes its position. It is also called *Meratia præcox* and *Calycanthus præcox*. The following note shows with what enthusiasm the English gardener goes to his task, or did go when this ancient writer wrote: —

A deciduous shrub, native of Japan, remarkable for the fragrance of its flowers from December to March in the open, growing to a height of six feet or more as bushes, in sheltered situations and much higher against a wall. This is so very desirable a shrub, on account of the fragrance of its flowers and their being produced throughout the whole of the winter, that no garden should be without it. In the small plots in front of suburban street houses, it may be planted against the house and trained up so as to form a border to one or more of the windows. A few of the blossoms may be gathered daily and placed in the drawing-room or boudoir, the same as violets.[1]

The flowers come on new wood only, so it should be trimmed back severely in spring. It is perfectly hardy around Phila-

[1] Loudon's *Arboretum et Fruticetum*.

delphia, but often gets its buds frosted; so it may be added
that the bush honeysuckle (*Lonicera fragrantissima*) will give
the same pleasure and be much easier to procure. Some
branches, brought into the house in March, burst at once
into bloom and are deliciously scented. The bush is, however, quite rampant, and will eventually take up much
space; it should also be trimmed severely.

Doronicum (leopardbane) is another of the bright daisy-
like flowers of the early year. It is also a disappearing-after-
blooming plant and is apt to get "dug over" by the handy
man's fork. I do not consider it a very lasting inhabitant;
though I propagated a quantity by means of rootstocks for
several years, it has now departed, as I did not keep my
mind on it. There are two varieties, *D. austriacum* and *D.
caucasicum*. Their rootstocks are perennial and both are easily
cultivated in any good garden soil, but they prefer a rather
heavy one and a dampish place.

Fritillaria I approach with delight and the pleasure of long
acquaintance, at least with two of the species. John Weathers,
in his Bulb book, says there are forty-one; I have tried but
three. Of these, *F. recurva* was a charming scarlet nodding
bell that soon swung or rang its life away. This was one of
the Americans of the family. There are several procurable
from California, their native home: *F. purdyi*, of open fields
and heavy clay soil, and *F. coccinea*, *pudea*, and *recurva* of
shady woods.[1] But the two most usually found in gardens
are *Fritillaria meleagris* (guinea-hen flower, the snake's-head
fritillary or checkered daffodil), and *F. imperialis*, the crown-
imperial of legend — and also of repellent odor, like that of
the fox or skunk. In the Dutch bulb lists before Quarantine

[1] Bailey's *Encyclopedia of Horticulture*.

37, *F. imperialis* was usually put first, with no explanation as to size or characteristics, it was so well known over there, and I often thought *F. meleagris* was overlooked for its more showy relation. I once told a friend who wanted the dainty dark bells of meleagris and its white variety that fifty would be quite enough for her small town garden. So off went her list without her specifying which, — or perhaps she took the first one on the list, — and she was overwhelmed with fifty of the enormous bulbs of *F. imperialis*. The following spring she was again overwhelmed with their odor, decidedly overpowering in a city walled plot. A Virginian writes of the stunning sight the crown-imperial made in an old garden down there, and I fancy a fox-hunting squire of England or Virginia would enjoy his evening cigar mingled with the reminiscent odor of the chase, but it is wiser to place it far away from the house, where the stately beauty of the golden or orange bells on stalks of handsome foliage three or four feet high may be distantly enjoyed. The pure yellow variety is very good, and all are long-lived plants. The legend is that they grew in the garden of Gethsemane and were the only flowers that refused to bow their heads when our Saviour walked by. Hence they have been forever condemned to turn their bells downward.

Fritillaria meleagris and its variety *alba* are but one half to one foot high. When I first saw these marvelously formed flowers in my garden, a thrill of wonder passed through me that always recurs each spring when they nod their bells in the wind. The name "snake's head" too is well chosen, if one notes the way they appear from the ground — a manner of stealing along, then an upward lift with the bud still sheathed in its green case, then the final lift erect; all is most

suggestive of a snake. And the snake, in the garden lore of
Persia and in their ancient pictures of gardens, is always
used as a symbol of spring. W. H. Hudson has written in his
Book of A Naturalist a description of a field of the brown
checkered fritillary; he also speaks of the wonder that it
excites, and says that the older writers on plants waxed
eloquent in describing their fritillaries or ginny flowers; that
it is a flower, which once seen, cannot be forgotten. And
this is because of its unlikeness to all others, its strangeness.
He is speaking then of the dark ones, but to many the white
variety is the most beautiful: "A tulip without its stiffness,
but pendulous like the harebell." The faint green tracery
on the white petals adds to its charm. Both these forms of
F. meleagris naturalize easily and love a deep, rather heavy,
damp soil, where they increase readily for me.

Many of our favorite flowers have been immortalized by
English poets from Shakespeare downward. The primrose,
daisy, violet, and daffodil have had many melodious changes
rung upon them. But the fritillary has the unique distinction
of appearing only once so far in any verse by our greater
poets. Matthew Arnold, whose poetry possesses such depth
and quiet charm, has achieved the difficult feat of finding a
rhyme for "fritillary." Anyone who has seen the meadows
at Christchurch, Oxford, when the thousands of fritillaries
are blooming and who also knows this verse of "Thyrsis,"
will never forget the guinea-hen flower.

> I know what white, what purple fritillaries
> The grassy harvest of the river fields
> Above by Ensham, down by Sanford, yields,
> And what sedged brooks are Thames's tributaries.

Helleborus niger (the Christmas rose) may be had in bloom

Fritillary meleagris, the guinea-hen flower; of low growth, it differs from its taller relation F. imperialis, the crown-imperial

from December to March and is such a treasure that every gardener grows covetous when it opens its blooms on a cold winter day, yet few take trouble enough the following July to prepare a bed for it. The wise possessor will rarely risk division, even to her nearest and dearest, for *Helleborus niger* is a superior plant and resents being tampered with, preferring to remain on an entailed estate, as it were, where peace and quietness will be assured. Reginald Farrer, in *The English Rock Garden*, puts an inimitable phrase about it: "*H. niger*, so called because its heart or root is black, while its face shines with a blazing white innocence unknown among the truly pure of heart." And "*H. niger* is one of the candors of the world." This seems going rather far in discussing a mere plant, but it is quite justified. I have no bed of flawless hellebores, though I have the graves of two and the seeds of four — these last are a challenge that shall come to fruition. I know well, however, a planting by a friend's house that has been there twenty years or more and is a wondrous sight to see on a December day, and I remember, too, one foggy night at February's end, they were still showing spotless cups and golden stamens amid their handsome leaves. Darnell lists fourteen members of the genus, some having several varieties. *Helleborus niger* (var. *altifolius*) is by far the best. *H. maximus* is often confounded with it. *H. angustifolius* has smaller snowy white flowers, and H. Madame de Fourcade is a very fine garden form.

Helleborus orientalis is called "the Lenten rose," and has been freely hybridized with other species. This has blossoms over two inches across, rose colored with pale green shadings. It is this one that has been mostly propagated by nurseries in the United States. The Federal Horticultural Board is now asking amateurs to import any and all hellebores they wish, offering them easy permits, as there is so little stock in this country. They need a deep, rather sandy loam with leaf mould in a semishaded spot. The English writer, Darnell, advocates their facing west, but over here they would be at the mercy of the cutting harsh winds from that direction. It is imperative that they should be near the house, just off the porch or terrace, where one can enjoy them, and cover, if needed, to keep storms from soiling the flowers. The roots are numerous, thick and fleshy, almost tuberous like those of the dahlia. In some old gardens one sees the red-purple form, probably *H. olympicus* from Eastern Europe. Others are, *H. abschasicus, antiquorum, atrorubens, caucasicus, colchicus, corsicus, cupresus, fœtidus, guttatus, lividus, odorus.*

Leucojum — say the word very fast and one is reminded of Lewis Carroll and "The snark was a boojum, you see"; say it slowly and you will be learning the name of one of the loveliest bulbs of spring, one that you may have three bites of a cherry from, so to speak: *L. vernum* in March, *L. carpaticum* in April, and *L. pulchellum* in May, though at present, with the quarantine, you will be lucky to get just one kind and will never be positive which one, unless you already possess the others for comparison. The blossoms of *L. vernum* are so anxious to be up to give the bees their very first drink that they push their white bells out almost with the leaves, which commence to show their tips in February and even earlier. In places sheltered at the north and west they are quite long in stem, as tall as the larger snowdrops, which everyone thinks they are until you point to the utterly different shape. Their white petals are green or yellow-tipped on the edge, and they have not the inner bell that the snowdrop has. *L. carpaticum* is taller and comes a little later, while *L. pulchellum* in May is about a foot tall and has often several bells to a stalk and several stalks to a bulb. Many of these leucojums grow in old Southern gardens, especially around Charleston, so will be available. They are called spring snowflakes, as well as snowdrops, indiscriminately.

Shortia galacifolia has a romantic history though a very prosaic name. It was discovered in North Carolina in 1788 by André Michaux, the famous French botanist. It was lost for a century as Michaux went back to France with but one dried specimen and one berry. He had never seen it in flower. It lay nameless and forgotten until our American botanist Asa Gray was in Paris in 1839, studying Michaux's collection, and the label caught his eye: From "les hautes montagnes de Caroline." Something about the drawing and the dried specimen attracted Dr. Gray and he determined to hunt for it on his return. He made two unsuccessful trips to the region described by Michaux; it was finally found in 1886 by the late Professor Charles Sprague Sargent of the Arnold Arboretum and a party of botanists. They at once sent a box of it to Dr. Gray. It was named for Dr. Short, a distinguished Southern naturalist, and subtitled *galacifolia*, as it resembled the galax in leaf. It has now been propagated for many years and, though a bit difficult to grow, is a goal for the skillful gardener. It likes to have acid soil and to be tucked a little beneath a shady rock in a moist place.

Anyone who has gardened long and widely and wisely can prolong this list indefinitely.

VI

A DECORATIVE SPRING CLIMBER

LOVE born of knowledge, love that gains
Vitality as Earth it mates.
"A Reading of Earth," GEORGE MEREDITH

ONCE, in an old bookshop that was a haunt of mine, a slim little volume, hardly large enough to be graced with such a ponderous name, attracted me by its title — *The Virgin's Bower*. This may suggest a garden resting place for a spinster aunt and her meditations, but, as the little book lay on a shelf labeled GARDENS — HORTICULTURE, it seemed to be a good gamble and it was promptly purchased. It proved to be a dissertation on varieties of clematis by William Robinson, of Gravetye, that dean of English gardening. All sorts, all varieties of this charming vine, its propagation and treatment, were here set forth in detail, while exquisite sepia photogravures accompanied the text.

Our native clematis, *C. virginiana*, and the Japanese variety, *C. paniculata*, had long been in my possession. Planted at the base of a row of cedar posts, they festooned themselves on strands of wire between the pillars. In late August and early September their bloom made a soft snowstorm effect, and the fragrance penetrated every corner at dusk. On moonlight nights it made the garden eerie and fairylike. But the large-flowered sorts were unknown to me, except the purple *C. jackmani*, which was invariably planted to climb over the walls of the red-brick houses that made Philadelphia the "city of homes" in the early nineties — but oh, such ugly ones! The two colors had always seemed to me particularly hideous together, — this was before the day of the "impressionists," — yet even now my eye fails to see beauty in the juxtaposition of red brick and purple *C. jackmani.*

Clematis montana had been bought when it first came out, a debutante in the catalogues, though planted in a position where it was often so killed back in winter that it was discouraged from blooming at its normal early date. With this small experience, and never planting it in a more favored place, its newer and much vaunted variety, *C. montana rubens,* was never tried. Alas! how backward we are, how stupid in letting the years pass when we might be planting and trying again and again, so that we might prove irrevocably success or failure! Too late! The years grow fewer, until we can but garden in spirit, or sadder yet, return as ghosts to our beloved garden plots, only to find Nature has spread her lavish coverlid of weeds upon our efforts and little or nothing remains.

William Robinson of Gravetye, like our own intrepid late Charles Sargent of the Arnold Arboretum, has no such fears for the future of his plantings. Like most of us true gardeners, he never thinks of it in connection with himself. Hale and hearty in mind, though now quite old and able to go about only in a wheeled chair, he constantly plants new varieties of everything, and tries them out.

Thus with the genus Clematis. "We make," he says, "a good deal of clematis at Gravetye." And indeed they must. Reading in *The Virgin's Bower* — and always this delightful title lures me afresh — what this master gardener had accomplished, the possibilities of what I might do, even with my amateur and too often careless hands, became unlimited, and my courage rose and enthusiasm kindled. Seeing in New England some pillar posts glorious with huge saucer-like flowers of a pale lavender, and learning it was *Clematis Ramona*, it was forthwith ordered and planted. Too soon it died; again it was bought, this time from a more northern nursery, where hardiness might be hoped for. It grew, and throve, and bloom began to come. The effect was good, but it left the old post too bare in winter, for though this clematis does not die down to its root each winter, as some do, it drops its leaves. So Euonymus was tried most successfully (the variety *vegetus*) which gives the red berries in autumn. The euonymus serves also as a support for the clematis and a protection. Now, after six or seven years' growth, Ramona climbs and climbs, and by the end of May — still within the confines of spring — she flames and glows up one side of the arbor, opening her large flowers until the leaves are hidden from top to bottom. One may say "flames" with strict truth, for flame is blue, and in the sunset light one gets all the other colors of fire in the sky. With the deep green glossy leaves of the euonymus as a background, Ramona is a bit of beauty. I hazard a guess — which is not a wise thing to do in a serious work of horticulture — that this Ramona, though not so named in the catalogue of the firm whence I bought, is *C. lanuginosa* or a hybrid of it. William Robinson calls this the noble virgin's-bower, the best of the large-flowered kinds, sent by Robert Fortune from the north of China. The white and pale wine-colored varieties, Henryi, Duchess of Edinburgh, and Madame Edouard André, were planted after William Robinson's fashion. "We use," he says, "slender oak or chestnut poles [I used bamboo canes]

Clematis montana rubens, covering a stone seat in the garden of a friend

to train them up against the fir trees on which they love to climb, and then, when they fling their large white or colored flowers through the branches, the dark background makes a fine foil for them." This in the case of the old Japanese variety *paniculata* had been going on in my garden for years, unplanned, as many of one's best effects often are, yet noted and encouraged a little by my guiding hand. Just enough to keep the pruning shears away, and remembering to harangue the hired man when he attempted the so-called "cleaning out," as he did one winter, cutting down a climbing rose that had attained unbelievable heights in a no-good-for-fruit old pear tree.

The ancient fallacy that vines kill trees should be amended to "some vines do." The slender growth of the clematis — the large-flowered kinds — could not possibly hurt the old spruce trees that I planned to be their support. Once a hedge of these had edged the north side of the garden; a few were left when the wall was built, and on these the experiment was tried. Four various colored hybrids were bought and placed in spring. Hopes high were soon prostrated as the vines prostrated themselves also one by one. Once more going farther north to buy, again they were planted, though with the loss in time of a whole year between. For one always expects they will — as they sometimes do — shoot up from the root again. And if one's plant is on its own roots, one is safe; if grafted, it will take another whole year to make sure what you have. Next we learned, but not from William Robinson, that in England it is the custom to sink a pot of rose geranium or some such finely cut foliage plant at the base of the clematis, thus giving the required shade to its lower parts. There seems to be some potency too in the rose geranium, as that is the one always mentioned, and this year, when I neglected putting one on my west-side planted clematis, the creature sulked and died down. The cat was blamed, but it may have been temperament; for now the rose geranium is there, the vine is putting up new shoots. Before its untimely fainting fit it had climbed up — this one is on a wall — some ten feet and had given flowers the same number of *inches* across. They have been marvelous for two years, supposed to be the variety Duchess of Edinburgh. The second time the ones on the four fir trees were planted, they behaved well. Their labels were, however, illusive, and all turned out precisely alike, though purchased for four different varieties. Labeling is still in its infancy in our United States.

These large-flowered clematis are hardy on a north wall too; indeed, safer there, as they are cooler during our hot summers. Give them a good-sized hole filled with compost, leaf mould predominating, and they will do wonders anywhere. But the happiest spot of all, as William Robinson well knew when he wrote his little book, is clambering up and through an evergreen, if it is not too dense a one and has a somewhat slender trunk, bare of branches part way up. Place the plant well away from the trunk, of course, so it may get its food from the well-prepared hole, and give it in its early growth the needed help of the bamboo stake. They also do well trained over a stone balustrade, where the nodes of the vine may get the warm, life-giving sun of early spring to swell the buds and leaves and tendrils that come from every joint. In such a place, *C. montana rubens* gave an especially glorious sight this last May in a friend's garden. The effect was that of large apple blossoms or huge anemones,

Clematis Ramona in May

as the flowers, some three inches across, were white, edged
and tinged with pink rather than the red one is led to expect
from the catalogues. *C. montana* too sets its flowers so
closely one sees no leaves at all. It should have a conspicuous
place in the spring picture.

Clematis tangutica, the Russian virgin's-bower, has, Mr.
Robinson says, large deep-yellow flowers, and should be tried
in bold ways over rocky slopes. It can be gotten in this
country. The old-fashioned purple-bell one, *C. crispa*, is nice
near the porch or terrace, where one can get its lily-of-the-
valley fragrance at night. This and *C. coccinea*, the scarlet-
flowered one from Texas, as well as several other kinds, are
our own native plants and could be hybridized to give many
lovely forms for our gardens, so that we might, as they do at
Gravetye Manor, pluck thirty sorts of wild and cultivated
clematis flowers in one day.

One way to use these beautiful and decorative large-
flowered varieties has been long in my mind. Though I have
not been able to give it a trial, it is practical, I am sure. Use
the chestnut woven fence that has been so often suggested
for the little garden's barrier. Plant these clematis on the
shady side if practicable. Fasten their growth carefully and
get them to the top as early as possible in spring. Then they
will drape the upper line of the fence and show off their
blossoms most charmingly. Euonymus may be planted in
conjunction — yes, should be, as it makes such a good
support, as well as protection and foil, for them. Get pot-
grown plants of the clematis from a nursery farther north,
as they will then come to you in a dormant state and have a
better chance to sprout under their future home conditions.

VII

WALL TRAINING FOR SHRUBS

WE think there are few scenes in an ornamental garden or
pleasure ground of greater interest to a person having a knowledge of botany, however slight, than a conservative wall.

LOUDON's *Arboretum* (1838)

IN my grandfather's library were many botanical books.
Some were forlorn-looking and aged, some were shabby as to
bindings, and some were falling apart. Therefore an unbook-
ish, unbotanical aunt had relegated many to the garret, as
the attic is called in old Chester County, Pennsylvania —
this same old county that is called the garden spot of the
world by some of its overoptimistic inhabitants. And herein
lies the significance of the worn-out books and the garden
spot; one caused the other. As for the attic, soon there will
be neither attic nor garret in the new toy-village houses, and
we shall have to have a glossary to explain the term.

During the process of many spring house-cleanings and of
many unbotanical generations growing up in the old house,
the poor books evidently had a desperate time, being pushed
aside while other tastes, other manners in print usurped their
places on the shelves. Then came the day I discovered one
relic, full of delightful facts and leisurely imaginings, Loudon's *Arboretum et Fruticetum Britannicum*. Its title page of
the year 1838 informed me there were seven other companion
volumes. Alas, where? The garret must be reëxplored. This
one first volume, however, proved to be a veritable plum
pudding of information, for Mr. Loudon explained at great

length what he purposed to do in all the forthcoming seven, and minced no words. Sonorous and glowing they rolled on. And suddenly it was as if my grandfather were present. Remembering George Meredith's lines, "To a friend lost": —

> For surely are you one with the white host,
> Spirits, whose memory in our vital air
> Through the great love of Earth they had: lo, these —

and as if he, happy in finding at least one descendant sharing his hobby, were directing me to a subject that had long interested me, though of it I knew little. For, idly turning the pages, I saw this alluring phrase, "a conservative wall." "Ah," thought I, "we of the new country, we of 1928, consider walls, garden walls, a sign of progressive gardening; what can the old Briton mean? Perhaps a wall of conservative length as regards its cost." This flash of insight on my part was most natural, as our long-hoped-for wall had perforce become more conservative, both as regards length and height, than we expected. For we saw the mason at one dollar per sixty minutes waiting daily and leisurely for his helper, who received half this amount per sixty minutes, and without whom the mason would not lift his trowel. Waiting for this helper, who seemed never to arrive except on rainy days, time passed; whereupon they would both lay off and disappear into the mist. Then, when paid their magnificent sums per day or week, a grand orgy of post-prohibition stuff would again lay them off for several — and always, it seemed, sunshiny — days. In 1838, I wondered, did masons assume these lordly airs? Oh, no; in Mr. Loudon's book, marquises, baronets, and all such beings exercise their rightful prerogatives and mere masons are not mentioned at all, yet how necessary they were! Consider the Marquess of Blandford,

whose place, "White Knights," was chiefly remarkable for
its magnolia wall, which was one hundred and forty-five feet
long and twenty-four feet high, entirely covered with twenty-
two plants of *Magnolia grandiflora*, which flowered every year
from June until November. And on another page, "But price
was never taken into consideration by the Marquess of
Blandford." There is the lordly manner for you, and the
right one, though we must admit we are not surprised when
farther down the page we read, "He found himself involved
in debt and lawsuits, which have greatly crippled his exer-
tions." But then, we reflect, he had the wall. But was that a
conservative wall? We perceive it was, and again it was not.
As we turn the pages idly backwards, a Chinese fashion of
reading that is our habit and a very useful one, for one gets
such a comprehensive and gradually illuminating view in this
way, we find Mr. Loudon's enthusiastic, glowing account of
what really is a conservative wall, and we too grow thrilled,
and vow to have this perfect and indispensable adjunct to
our beloved garden.

He begins by explaining the scope of his next division of
his contemplated Work — they regarded a book seriously in
those days. He intends to "give a list of all the perfectly
hardy species of trees and shrubs at present cultivated in
Britain," and to this he intends "to add a list of plants which
have been found by cultivation to be half hardy in the climate
of London," and of others which from their native countries
and habits he thinks "not unlikely to prove so." He does
this for two purposes: "The first, because, by trying species
from all countries in the open air, some hitherto kept in
greenhouses may be found quite hardy," and cites that this
was the case with kerria, cydonia, and hydrangea. The

second reason is, "that we think there are few scenes in an
ornamental garden or pleasure ground of greater interest to a
person having any knowledge of botany, however slight, than
a conservative wall; that is, a wall covered with trees and
shrubs, natives of foreign climates, which though they may
be killed to the ground during winter yet exhibit a degree of
luxuriance during the summer season, which they never can
display in our greenhouses . . . When we take into consideration how easy it is to have such walls flued (!) and to heat
the borders in front of them by small pipes of hot water, the
capacities of a conservative wall and border appear great
beyond anything we can at present calculate on; and we are
persuaded that, were the subject of conservative walls warmly
taken up by a spirited and wealthy individual, something
would be produced in this way as superior to our present
greenhouses and conservatories as these are to the orangeries
and greenhouses of the time of Evelyn, or even of Miller."

We thrill to that sentence, "Were the subject taken up by
a spirited individual" — alas, to have lived too late! I feel
myself capable of having been that person in 1838, unham-
pered then by any thought of masons and their costly hours
and minutes. But even now, in 1928, we may still have the
spirit, and we can use our own house wall, or our fence, hedge,
fedge, or what not, to train and trim our shrubs upon. Hardy
ones or half hardy, we get an undreamed-of return in bloom.
For we also, as did Loudon, grow our shrubs on walls for
several reasons: to get more bloom out of the shrub and to
take up less room than when grown in the usual way. This
last is an imperative reason in the little garden. A shrub is
often more decorative on a wall, and will give endless interest
and occupation for the shears. There is always a determined

shearer and trimmer in the family who is invariably dangerous. Give him or her a wall shrub or an espaliered tree for private use, and the trimmer will become completely absorbed in its growth and your other precious plants will be safe from possible depredations.

One does not have to have a walled garden to attempt this experiment. The house wall, if free from overhanging eaves, will do as well if the earth is deeply prepared. If there is a flagstone terrace close up to the house, see that a flag or two is taken away from against the wall and the space dug out to a foot or more and filled in with good soil. This has to be done — this deep digging and preparing at the base of any wall where planting is projected, for it is surprising how many stones, chips, clinkers, and other uncomfortable hard materials the builder leaves behind him.

If one has the garden enclosed with the chestnut woven fence, shrubs may be trained on it just as well, though they will not be so protected from the cold winds of spring and may not bloom so profusely. On the other hand, they will pass through our blistering summers better than if they had a reflecting surface back of them, if they are in full sun. We shall use only the hardiest varieties for first experiments. One of the easiest is forsythia. It blooms on the new wood of the previous summer, as almost everyone knows but the jobbing gardener who in March trims off its flowers-to-be, and it is more showy than *Jasminum nudiflorum*, which it somewhat resembles in bud, though it is not so rampant a grower. After you decide on your main stems and fasten them in a fan pattern on the wall, watch the new shoots in spring and shorten them as soon as they are a few inches long, when they will straightway branch again and you repeat the shortening, the idea being to get a mass of short new shoots all over the space between the main stems. These new shoots will all flower the next spring and should be cut off at once after blooming and the new shoots treated as before. It grows very rapidly, so after flowering the shearer can commence at once.

Another easy and very beautiful shrub for a wall is *Cydonia japonica*, the old-fashioned *Pyrus japonica* of our grandmother's dooryard. The variety *C. maulei* is a lovely apricot-pink and gives a stunning effect on gray stone. It is leggy in growth and is apt to send out suckers. As it flowers on old wood, one must trim judiciously, leaving enough to mature for bloom each year. It flowers in any kind of soil, and some of mine on a rocky dry bank far surpass the ones along the stream which is supposed to suit them. Inside a wall facing south, and under a pear tree there, they bloom too, so I conclude they do so anywhere and am trying them on a north wall now.

One would hardly recognize *Prunus triloba flore pleno*,[1] the double-flowering plum, when in bloom on a wall. It is a shower of pink. *Prunus tomentosa*,[1] the Chinese cherry that the Department of Plant Introduction has been popularizing the last few years, is especially charming to possess, as it pushes its buds out very early and its long wand-like branches covered with tiny pussy-willow-like buds, white flushed with pink, are so very different from the other flowering trees. A light running vine such as the large-flowered *Clematis jackmani* or *henryi*, placed near this, would not hurt it a whit,

[1]"Prunus" is used for both plum and cherry, according to Bentham and Hooker. See *The Manual of Trees of North America* by Charles Sprague Sargent.

and using the Prunus branches for support would give there a later flowering of fine color, if one of the good velvety purples or pale wine-pinks were used. I have a *Clematis paniculata*, certainly not a light but rather a heavy vine, growing over my *Prunus tomentosa;* it blooms in its usual luxuriant way and waning summer turns its great fluffy panicles of white to soft silky ones as the seed pods form. Through these, in September, glow the tiny scarlet cherries of the Prunus, giving as lovely an effect as the pink-white buds of spring.

An early-blooming shrub that requires a wall to bring its flower to perfection, though it is perfectly hardy, is the wintersweet, well known in England as *Chimonanthus fragrans*. But it led me a wandering chase among our nurserymen here, who have their own way of labeling. One February a twig was brought from the University of Pennsylvania to a botany class. Its small brownish-yellow bud gave out a delicious fragrance and everyone wanted to plant it. "But where can we get it?" No one knew, for the bush at the University had been planted many years before. After writing diligently north, south, east, and west, it was finally found under the name, *Meratia præcox*, and purchased in Oregon. It is a very straggly, awkward bush, so one in a sunny spot would be enough; walls are so precious, there are so many nice things to do with them and to put on them, one must be cautious. Do not put the wrong plant in, as I did on a south wall. It was part of our old barn and almost as high as the Marquess of Blandford's magnolia one; there I put a lusty rose, *Moschata alba*, a perfect, fragrant one, but so prickly and soon too big to transplant. One wants the south side for early bulbs and the wallflowers that may or may not live over our treacherous winter, and for late chrysanthemums, and flat against it the carefully-trained, well-clipped shrubs. Where the chrysanthemums are to go, one would put an autumn-blooming shrub, such as the rarely seen *Vitex agnus-castus* or chaste tree. This is a sparse bloomer in the open, but has charming soft blue spikes against a wall, and one would want here too the *Pyracantha angustifolia* with its orange berries and the *Cotoneaster horizontalis*, that will fan up a wall as well as hang over a rock bank. On the north side we would also train the syringa, — the early type, *Spiræa prunifolia* or bridalwreath, — and kerria, single and double. These three old companions, as shrubs, take up so much room one will be delighted with their restrained habits on a fence or wall. The shears must be kept active, however, as they grow, grow, grow after their April and May outburst of flowers. Many other kinds may be tried and they come crowding into mind as one reviews the familiar yearly repeated lists of the nurserymen. There is the tamarisk; it loves heat and drought, its feathery foliage is good, and its pink feathers of flower in midsummer would be interesting. Then there is *Viburnum carlesi*, suddenly grown costly and rare because its heavenly fragrance, unnoticed by the trade, was commented upon by some of our deans of horticulture, and the growers forthwith elevated its price into the exotic class; yet it is easy and hardy.

This is all a very far cry from dear old Loudon's *Arboretum et Fruticetum* and the conservative wall, yet that was only ninety years ago.

Have we made such far strides in gardening, after all? Have we not rather fallen back, in our stereotyped, follow-the-leader plantings of the same tree, the same shrub as our neighbor's, placed in the same way? Where is the spirited individual for whom Loudon longed? We answer, there are many, and they are everywhere, experimenting, trying out new plants and new methods, and not following their neighbor in anything unless he too has been awakened by the spirit of gardening finely.

VIII

PROPAGATING PROPAGANDA

EVERY child who has gardening tools,
Should learn by heart these gardening rules:
....
Though to shift, or to pot, or annex what you can,
A trowel's the tool for child. woman, or man.

JULIANA HORATIA EWING

THERE is nothing mysterious in propagating. The subject seems to be tabooed among amateur gardeners in America. We are becoming such a pampered people, everything must be boxed up in attractive packages and sent to our doors in glistening, gaily painted motors with liveried messengers, or we will have none of it.

To stop a bit in our mad rush for dear knows what, and going one knows not where, to stop a little and bide at home, *chez nous*, by the *foyer*, — in this instance, the back yard, — is not to be thought of. Hence one hears, "Oh, gardening is *so* expensive! Why, I spent fifty dollars on bedding plants for that border before I knew it. No, I cannot afford a hundred of those, much as I love them." These are remarks too frequent among us. It takes a little time to propagate, and it may take a little more time to make propagating popular. (Alliteration seems inevitable when upon this subject.) It may also strike terror to the nurseryman to have his secrets known, if secrets there are to anything so simple, but I do not think so; they can hardly keep up with the demand as it is, and there will always be people who want it *now*, and who did not or could not take time by the forelock.

One need not have much space. Concentration of mind as well as of ground is the requisite. One easy way of mine, for the quantities of forget-me-nots, English daisies (*Bellis perennis*), violas, and pansies needed, is, when giving the last weedings and clearings in autumn, to collect the tiny seedlings appearing all about, and plant them thickly in lines in a cold frame. Lacking a frame, empty boxes turned over them would do almost as well. Or a box with both bottom and top knocked out and a piece of glass placed over, would do. I prefer light on them, and one can look at them occasionally. Of course these stray waifs of pansies and violas may not be, probably won't be, fine varieties, but one is sure of having plenty to set out, or for early cutting. Forget-me-not (var. *dissitiflora*) soon seeds itself and becomes an habitué of the entire garden.

Foxgloves in this latitude must always be kept in a frame over winter, — small plants from August sowing or October gleaning, — wallflowers and pansies also, to be set out in April. *Phlox divaricata*, shredded apart, as said before, and put in rows after blooming must be set out in September so they may have time to get firmly rooted before winter, or kept till spring in the same row, no covering needed.

Primrose polyanthus, veris, and *vulgaris* must be divided in June after flowering. Pull apart each clump; they will come away easily into separate plants; each crown, the knotty part from which the leaves spring, will have enough roots to make a new plant at once. If they do not come away easily, cut with a sharp knife, leaving some roots to each piece of crown. Plant in a shady place and soak occasionally during summer with the hose. Any that are still very small by autumn, cover with a box, or transplant to a flat and put in a frame, or put directly in a frame in soil close up to glass. The ones outside, cover with salt hay, which it pays to buy, it is such a comfort to have for plants that might otherwise be smothered by too heavy a winter blanket, such as strawy manure or leaves which are apt to mat and spoil the crown. This applies to foxgloves also and other rosettelike plants which hold their leaves part of the winter. All the polyanthus primroses have the terrible habit of jumping high out of their places when the frost heaves the ground in spring, so one must go around then, pushing them back by the collar over and over again, or one will find the tiny ones lying full out on the ground, waving their bare roots in the air, like naughty children who have kicked their covers off.

Oriental poppies, Japanese anemones, *Phlox suffruticosa* Miss Lingard, — so apt to die out, this last, — and anchusa are easy. In autumn dig up a clump, cut its roots in two- or three-inch-long pieces, put in a cold frame in sandy soil, or else in a flat in a frame. In planting, be sure to keep the roots right side up, that is, the end toward the plant as you cut it is the top. In spring all will be sprouting young plants.

Dicentra spectabilis (bleedingheart) is very easily increased. It is also another of those "disappearing-after-blooming" plants. One may think it needs coddling, but what it really wants is to be absolutely forgotten. Very amusing too is the way it *was* forgotten by our nurserymen until the term "old-fashioned perennials" became their slogan. Then was Dicentra brought out, reinstated, and a neat little halo set about it of "difficult to procure on account of the quarantine," to enhance its value. Never a whisper got about that it was easy to propagate. Long ago there was a flagstone walk down the east side of the house I know so well. Along this walk were alternate clumps of peonies and bleeding-hearts. They rose in spring together from the ground, sturdy pink-red shoots of peony, slender pale green fronds of Dicentra. Soon the pink lyre-shaped flowers hung upon their arching stems, long before the peonies had set their buds. We children made earrings of them and dolls with hoop skirts. Soon the whole plant yellowed and vanished and we never noticed, being occupied with some other game, possibly that of sniping the first strawberries, while between the peonies Dicentra was discreetly dying, hidden by their foliage. Long years after, when I was gardening seriously, I dug up a curious, fungous-looking substance in late autumn on the lawn. It had buds on it like the eye of a potato or peony. Suddenly it struck me I had sliced into an old clump of bleedingheart, so a bit or two was planted inside the garden and the rest replaced where I had stumbled upon it. The next spring two fine plants appeared from those pieces. Since then I have made rows of Dicentra; it increases almost too fast between the peonies now, so digging and dividing is to its taste.

Cuttings of many shrubs placed in pure sand in a cold frame will be rooted or callused, so rooting is easy by spring. Yet how few of us make our own shrubs, even of pussy willows! Bunches of these bought on the streets are thrown out after a few weeks, their white roots in the vase showing their eagerness to be out on their own again.

All kinds of Dianthus root easily in autumn when the damp nights begin, if pieces pulled away from the parent plant are placed where wanted in gravelly soil, pressing the ground firmly. Many of the ground covers do this too, for instance, *Teucrium pyrenaicum*, an especially attractive low-growing one, with shiny leaves of darkest green. One needs quantities of plants when one starts a ground cover, and this and all the thymes are invaluable.

Euonymus is easy from cuttings in sand at any time of year, and even in open ground in a trench in very early spring. And who that has ever had a good berrying variety has not wanted more? E. var. *vegetus* is the berrying one, but the others make a fine wall-covering anywhere. June and July cuttings of many flowering shrubs will root in sand in a frame kept close, that is, covered with glass and a cotton cloth, on top, and with the sand kept wet. There are many little "dodges," as the Scotch gardener called them, and when one hears of any or reads of any, try them out and prove if they work, for, as William James discovered, this is the only true philosophy, the true pragmatism.

This propaganda should confine itself to spring plants, yet there are some autumn ones that so annoy me by disappearing each winter that I have formed a habit of taking a piece in time and making nine (plants), so I will include it here. There is Helenium, always apt to rot away in the middle so the whole clump vanishes, and *Boltonia latisquama*, the dainty pink one, and Heuchera, the alumroot. Of these, pieces are taken in the autumn with a bit of root attached, tucked into a double-sashed frame, left closed all winter, and there they are safe in spring, to be put out by the graves — most likely — of their former selves that have not survived.

But to return to spring propagation: many bulbs may be easily increased then; though the small-sized ones will not bloom for several years, one knows where they are, for they show up in March and may be transplanted as they bloom or just after, the little ones given more room. I have increased snowdrops to many thousands in this way, whenever the moment could be snatched to get the important bucket of sand to put a cushion under each little bunch as it is dropped into its new home. From this effort, clumps are now in delightfully unexpected spots; tall ones emerge from the leaf mulch of the rhododendron beds, and around tree trunks here and there. Short chilly-looking groups come up under lilac bushes and peonies from bare, uncovered soil, and in long, irregular rows in borders, and in many friends' gardens (I hope, for though the gifts have been made, perhaps they have been forgotten and not placed in the ground). Nay, nay, the friends to whom one entrusts tiny embryo souls, such as these tiny bulbs possess, are always too careful and appreciative gardeners to lose the gift!

With the leucojums (spring snowflakes) and the scillas (var. *nutans* and *campanulata*), it is safer to divide and transplant just after blooming. These two scillas should never be long out of the ground; they may go some five inches down and in shady places. It is difficult to tell which is right side up, they look so like small boiled new potatoes, yet if one inspects closely one sees the top is where the bulb within a bulb appears. *Scilla sibirica*, as we said before, is easy to multiply by picking them up as they lie like peas (of a pin's head size) on top of the ground after seeding time, or in autumn, when they still plainly show if the soil has not been stirred. Scratch the earth lightly under bush or tree where one wants a bright blue patch of color, scatter them thinly, and press some fine soil on them. They have a sort of prehensile tail which pulls them down to the necessary depth, as the crocus has — a provision of Nature as marvelous as all her works.

Thus and thus only may the gardener propagate easily and simply, by observing two rules: staying at home, and grasping the proper time and season for garnering the increase.

IX

THE PRIMULA FAMILY — SOME SPRING SPECIES

ALL the girls are out with their baskets for the primrose;
Up lanes, woods through, they troop in joyful bands.
"Love in the Valley," GEORGE MEREDITH

THE charm of a flower, a plant, is often, as we have said, so entwined and enmeshed in tradition that one accepts it and takes it for granted as one of the indispensables of the garden. Every Englishman, Scotchman, and Irishman may do this unconsciously in the case of the primrose, while the Englishman has not only his tradition, but his political affiliation often associated with it — that is, if he belongs to the Primrose League, formed to support the principles advocated by Disraeli, devoted subject of Queen Victoria, and named for his favorite flower. Many will remember when the actor George Arliss gave his memorable performances of "Disraeli," the large bowl of yellow (supposedly) primroses that always graced the table or desk near him. Yet perhaps only the tradition-lovers in the audience noticed this little floral touch.

But apart from all tradition, the primrose in all its species has a charm for many and has always appealed very poignantly to me. Every characteristic of the plant in every variety delights one; it is so neat in *Primula veris* and *acaulis*, so exquisite in leaf, all curled and fretted like a hugely magnified frond of parsley. And the fragrance of even its roots, when dividing them in autumn — for it has as strong a perfume there as the peony — awakens all the keen pleasure that its spring flowers give. Always the shades of yellow have been dearest to me, and even since growing many different colors and kinds, the pale yellow to orange ones have been my favorites. Yet the gold-laced polyanthas in velvety red have a quaint beauty too and are permanent residents in heavy soil. Of late years the great lavender and white balls of *P. denticulata*, the whorls of magenta and white *P. japonica*, and the magnificent species of China in marvelous shades of orange and salmon, have become almost as precious as the early yellows. The species *P. sieboldi* has aniline purple and white and lavender bracts, in form very like the *P. obconica* of winter greenhouses.

Taking the best known and best loved first, the common English primrose, let us make its distinction from the others clear. The names primrose, polyanthus, cowslip, oxlip are used loosely and inaccurately. I am indebted to Mr. Clarence Elliott of Stevenage, Herts, England, for the following elucidation, which he sent me through his cousin some years ago. I had imported Dr. MacWatts's book, *The Primulas of Europe*, on its first publication, but it is such a comprehensive work that it treats the English primrose a bit cursorily, or so I thought at the time; but on looking it over lately I find, interlarded between the botanical lists, quite a deal of information. He gives notes on culture, but not so full of detail as I had expected. Possibly all Scotchmen know these minor matters by instinct, but my Scotch strain had been too Americanized by climate and other things to grasp and learn by inference all that I had hoped to learn in black and white from his book. Mr. Elliott's table of contents, done by his manager, Ingwersen, who was, he wrote, a "first

rate" botanist, is absolutely understandable by the amateur.
It is headed: —

DISTINCTION OF PRIMROSE, COWSLIP AND OXLIP GROUP OF
PRIMULACEÆ — VERNALE
(Based upon the Work of Bentham and Hooker)

Species *Primula veris*, Linn. This is a collective name. It embraces 3 subspecies. Stock perennial, tufted. Leaves ovate or oblong, usually about 3 inches long, of a pale green, slightly toothed and much wrinkled. Calyx tubular, half an inch or more in length. Corolla usually yellow, the tube as long as the calyx or longer. The limb deeply five lobed. Each lobe shortly notched. Stamens within the tube (enclosed or just protruding).

(a) The Primrose, *P. vulgaris*, Hooker. *P. acaulis*, Linn.
More or less hairy. Peduncles apparently all radical, as long as the leaves, each bearing a single flower, with broad flat limb. Calyx teeth narrow and pointed.

(b) The cowslip or Paigle, *P. veris*, Linn. Not hairy, but often covered with a minute pale down. Flower stalks rising above the leaves, bearing a one-sided umbel of flowers. Calyx teeth usually broad and obtuse, rather inflated. Corolla with concave or cup-shaped limb. Very much smaller than the primrose, but varying in size.

(c) The Oxlip. *P. elatior*, Jacq. This is the plant commonly so-called in England, where the true plant only very rarely occurs in the eastern counties. This is entirely distinct from the following description. The plant I describe here under this name should really be called *P. variabilis*, I think.

P. elatior, vera. The Bardsfield or Normandy oxlip is common on the Continent in the north of France and in the Baltic provinces here and there, in the latter often in Beech woods close to the sea. It is very distinct indeed and very sweet scented. Flowers very pale yellow in a rounded umbel on a long peduncle, calyx not inflated, leaves hairy and mostly adpressed to the ground. The flower is smaller than the primrose, but much larger than in the finest cowslip I ever saw. This plant is scarcely known in England in gardens or in the wild state, but has, I believe, entered largely into the making of the modern Polyanthus. Whilst I strongly suspect that the false oxlip of England is very largely responsible for the so-called bunch primroses of gardens, with which it has the habit

in common of so often seeming a true colored primrose early in the
season and presently lengthening its peduncle and becoming practically a polyanthus. This is purely conjecture; there seem to be
no valid data on so old a favorite of our gardens. *P. vulgaris rosea*
and other eastern European forms of the primrose account for the
colors of garden primroses and bunch primroses as well as for the
old double primroses, and they have also doubtless entered in the
modern polyanthus in common with some of the colored forms of
the cowslip which occur rarely in England and more commonly on
the Continent. The only satisfactory way to prove this is to procure
a truly wild species and subspecies and color forms of them, and
make a long series of crosses, and recross the hybrids. A fine field
of study for a person of leisure and means.

Thus he ends, and that last phrase haunts one: "Of leisure
and means." We know of people with and without that last-
named possession, but of the first, "of leisure," none — no,
not one exists nowadays in this country. Truly an Englishman speaks.

Keeping these distinctions clear in mind, — of the primrose, cowslip, and oxlip,— we shall find that most of the
"English primroses" we buy in this country are the polyanthus, bunch-flowered type, hybrids, and that the more prized
ones have strong stout stems crowned with large umbels of
quite large flowers, sometimes an inch across, their colors
varying from yellow to orange and crimson. If we are not
collectors and not especially devoted to finding things out
botanically, we shall stop here, well satisfied, and only
demand that the gardener divide them occasionally and keep
the shady borders edged with them. But if we are primrose
lovers, this will not suffice. We shall track down the "single-
stem primrose." Taking the largest flowered of these, we shall
divide, transplant, and save the seed. *This* is the flower
of Wordsworth's lines, "A primrose by the river's brim a yellow primrose was to him" — and to us it is much, much

more. This is *P. vulgaris*, Hooker, *P. acaulis*, Linnaeus, and if your plant becomes polyanthus in its later flowering season, that is, if the flowers crowding up so thickly on their single stems are accompanied by other stronger stalks bearing at their tops a number of smaller flowers in an umbel, it is, as our botanist friend Ingwersen says, one that has become mixed with the false oxlip of England. The *P. elatior* I have also had, the true plant, as it was brought to me from fields around Havre, in northern France. It is smaller and shorter stemmed, the flowers star-shaped and very pale yellow, a dear creature, worthy of increase.

The cowslip or paigle, *P. veris*, Linn. — not hairy but "often covered with . . . down," came to me as lusty-looking "English primroses, field grown," bought by the hundred. Alas! I soon rued the day, as their lustiness increased and they threatened to seed all over the place. Their flowers were small, their peduncles so large, bunched on the end of the long stalk, they looked exactly like their name, "Peter's Keys," of the legend. Their one good attribute was fragrance, which is said not to belong to them, so they too may have been of mixed origin. One would think the true primrose would be found in Virginia, brought by the early colonists. Mine from there are small-flowered, in umbels on long stalks, the polyanthus type, *P. elatior* or *P. veris*.

As for cultivation, it takes a long time to learn their ways in this variable climate of the Middle Atlantic States, and in the most middle and most variable part of that map division. Most of the writers on Primula lore are of the three countries mentioned above, England, Ireland, and Scotland. What they do at Sligo Bay in Ireland, the success they have at Edinburgh's rock garden, and in Devon and Cornwall.

cannot be repeated in New York, Pennsylvania, and New Jersey. Our winters are never the same, as we have said before, nor are our summers, for that matter. We have several American primulas, but they all live out West and have no aroma of tradition about them; we want the alluring ones of "spring in England." We cannot invent methods of growing them without much subsequent trying out, by the "trial-and-error" rule. What I know of them is the result of grim experience, and I always want to hear of that of others, not so grim perhaps as mine. Yet out of mine has come some simple technique that may help beginners.

"Sow the seed as soon as ripe" is always told one, yet often it is months old before it reaches one from abroad. Seed of the wild primrose is very slow in germinating, like all the others of the Primulaceæ family. Keep the pan or box free from weeds. You will welcome many newborn ones after six months' waiting, and thereafter for twelve months they will continue to appear. Prick them off, as they form three to four leaves, into a fresh box, leaving the original one to go on germinating. Plant the seed in autumn. Leave the box in the open and pile snow on, when you can get it, during winter. If you are in a hurry, bring them into a coolish greenhouse after January, but the easiest way is to let them stand outside on ashes in a frame without glass. After the young plants have been pricked off to their new boxes of fairly light rich soil, they may be left severely alone on the north side of a bank or building where they will have shade part of the day and a dampish place. Look at them in dry weather and soak if necessary. This is simpler than planting them out where they may get smothered by grass. But if one is going away and no one watches them, it is safer to plant out in open ground. They root so firmly they are not easily crowded by weeds. The new young plants from these boxes will give their finest flowers the following spring, if transplanted their first autumn to a cold frame in October. Keep the glass on during severe winter weather, but ventilate. In April they will bloom earlier than those outside and give longer stems for picking. They may be lifted in full flower to the border or to pots for the house. The larger clumps may be divided in June — pulling the crowns apart — and planted in rows along the shady side of a building. The same treatment applies to *P. denticulata*, called *P. cashmeriana* by some dealers, though it is the same. These put out their lavender balls, composed of tiny florets in an umbel, on stout mealy stalks very early in April. They like damp places where their leaves will grow as long and large as those of the later candelabra species. They are extremely effective and very hardy, and can stand their fleshy roots running down into pure mud. The white variety is not so attractive, but is good for contrast.

Another spring species, that came to me as *P. veitchi*, is really *P. sieboldi*, a division of the Indian primroses and very like the greenhouse one so familiar to us in shops the winter through. It has some lovely white and lavender forms, but its prevailing color is bright magenta. It does well with partial shade and in leaf mould and light grass. Also I have seen it — to my surprise, I must confess — in quite dry spots on a rock garden. Its leaves vanish during summer and it has a creeping rootstock, so is difficult to keep in the border where it may get dug over.

The candelabra section, so called from the growth of its flower stalk, whorl upon whorl of bloom late in July, should

not come in a spring discussion. They need a book to themselves. They are also rather modern arrivals. My "Report
of the Primula Conference" of the Royal Horticultural
Society of 1913 hardly treats of their culture at all; they
were newcomers then, and though they, with *P. japonica*,
are now well known in England, they are not freely grown
here, where they are as completely at home as in Asia.
These, with *P. denticulata* and *P. sieboldi*, should be called by
the more stately name of "Primula," and we should keep
our dear "Primrose" title for our cowslips, oxlips, paigles,
and "beares-ears." Whence came these last two names?
Gerarde and Parkinson should tell us.

One rainy day in spring, it chanced that I found refuge in
a most perfect library, whose collection of priceless garden
books has quite possibly no rivals, for nowhere else could one
find an owner whose knowledge of gardening and of books
appertaining thereto is so nicely, so wisely, and so lavishly
balanced. The library was a perfect room, artistically and
architecturally, and in front of its great fireplace, I read and
noted these words from an ancient book of the year 1657,
Adam in Eden, or the Paradise of Plants, by William Coles: —

OF PRIMROSES, COWSLIPS AND BEARES-EARS

Primroses are usually called in Latine, Primula veris, because
they are the first that flourish in the Spring, or at least flourish with
the first nay sometimes they flourish all Winter if the weather be
calm. Both these and the cowslips are named Arthritics or Herbe
Paralysus, because they are good against the pains of the Joynts
and Sinews. In English Petty-Mulleins or Palsieworts, but most
commonly cowslips. The greatest sort are called for the most part
Ox-lips and Paigles.

Paigles — the Kinds. And here I might muster up a whole
regiment of the three sorts, but I shall mention no more at this time
than those I find spoken of by Gerarde, which are (1) the white

single or field primrose, (2) the purple primrose, which by the Turks is called carticheck, (3) the white double primrose, (4) the green primrose, (5) Field cowslip, (6) Field ox-lip, (7) double paigles, (8) cowslips, two in a hose (9) white Bird eine, (10) Red Birdeine (11) Yellow Bears Ears, (12) Purple Bears Ear, (13) Red Bears Ear, (14) Scarlet Bears Ear, (15) Blush Bears Ear, (16) Bright Bears Ear, (17) Stamel Bears Ear, (18) Little white Bears Ear.

He that desires to be better informed in these kinds of flowers [Is there anyone, I ask, after reading such a formidable list?] let him consult the masculine, but especially the feminine work of Mr. Parkinson, who hath treated of them more largely. There have been many sorts also found out and brought from beyond the seas of late daies. [And they have not ceased coming.]

Of all these names, one lingers over "Birdsein"; that one is nearly akin in homely endearment to our favorite primrose, and the tiny *P. farinosa* is still called the birdseye primrose. Reginald Farrer says that *P. farinosa*, "besides being the loveliest of our native Alpines [in England] has the widest distribution in the whole race. In all the alpine chains of the Northern Hemisphere the species, or forms very closely allied, are to be found, though it is but poorly represented in China, and not at all in the Himalayas. No gardener is a stranger to the wistful beauty of the "Pretty Bird e'en," with its little rosettes of gray and mealy foliage and its delicate scapes, all powdery white, carrying that loose round head of fragrant, soft pink flowers with a twinkling yellow eye. "It is easy," he says, "in grass, fine grass," and suggests that one sow *Festuca ovina tenuifolia* with it and "take no more care." On the other hand, Dr. MacWatt says, "Grass grows too rank," and that he has experienced no difficulty in growing it in ordinary soil. Thus the authorities differ! Farrer gives about one hundred pages to Primula in his monumental two volumes, *The English Rock Garden;* Dr. MacWatt's book is some two hundred pages long; and who am I that I should dare compete with them? Of Auricula too, I do not feel myself yet skillful enough to tell of my own experience. Dr. MacWatt treats quite fully of them. He considers them as Section 3 of the European Primula, the first comprising *P. vernale*, which include all we have been discussing under *P. elatior*, *P. acaulis*, and so on. *P. farinosa* is Section 2, and *P. auricula* Section 3. The outstanding difference of Auricula from Primula is that in almost all primulas the young leaves have their margins rolled backward when they first emerge from the bud, but in two sections, Floribunda and Auricula, the margins of the young leaves are rolled inward.

The origin of all the names for primrose, cowslip, and the like is interesting. Dr. MacWatt gives several instances. He says, "It comes as a surprise to the admirer of the primrose when he learns for the first time that the name was not always applied to our favorite flower but was at first indiscriminately used for the earliest spring plants. The privet would seem to have first claimed the title of primrose, and some early accounts which give us the title evidently applied to that shrub." Can he mean our ubiquitous hedge plant of the suburbs in the United States? Would that we could replace all privet with the gentle, smiling *P. acaulis!* Canon Ella-combe says, "Its name is one of the greatest puzzles to the etymologist." Dr. Prior says, "The old name was Prime Rolles or Primerole. Primerole is an abbreviation of Prim-everole; Italian '*Primaverola*,' diminutive of 'prima vera,' from 'flor di prima vera,' the first spring flower. Primerole, as an outlandish, unintelligible word, was soon familiarized into Primerolles and this into Primrose. But by Shakespeare's time the reference to Privet had been superseded and the name was firmly attached to the flower we love." Parkinson, Rea, and others all speak of the primrose as *Primula veris* or *Primula hortensis*, the cowslip being then generally called Paralysus. The name Paigle, occasionally applied to the cowslip, is still more difficult to trace, and philologists are hopelessly at sea respecting its origin. A suggestion has been made that it may have been derived from an old Scottish verb, "paigled," which means drooping with fatigue, and is said to have come from an Icelandic word, "piackur," drooping.

But what care we for the obscure origins of names, except in dull winter weather to while away an hour before the fire with books? On one of those heavenly days of early April, when contemplating my primrose meadow where lives my small collection in all tones of yellow and all members of the *P. vulgaris*, *P. acaulis* tribe, I think of ceasing every other occupation to devote myself to this one section alone. Always some cold frames, very cold ones, are filled with small plants, too small to trust out even under their salt-hay blanket. The cold frames, with the glass on in winter and through February and March, force the plants gently, and with other frames of forget-me-nots and pansies, they give long-stemmed flowers for cutting and a feeling that spring is here, long before she really comes.

Notes on Seed-planting and Soil for Auriculas and Primulas, that Should Suit the Most Meticulous Gardener
(From James Maddock's *Florist's Dictionary*, London, 1792)

Soil for Auriculas; ½ cow manure 2 years old, fresh sound earth of an open texture. Coarse sea or river sand. Soft decayed willow wood (from trunks of old willow trees). Peaty or moory earth. Ashes of burnt vegetables. In order to procure the last articles with very little trouble, any weeds, sticks, straws or old mats that are of no other value may be collected together in a heap and consumed by fire, in the open air, till the ashes become white; they will contain a small portion of alkali salts, which should be spread upon the surface of the other ingredients.

The compost is to be placed in an open situation, perfectly exposed to the action of both air and sun, from the influence of which it will derive great benefit; it should be turned over once or twice and as often pass through a coarse sieve that it may be well mixed. It should then be laid in a regular heap or mass, from 12 to 18 inches thick, but not more, and in this state it may remain a year before it is made use of, during which period it will be proper to turn it over two or three times, in order to expose all its parts to the atmosphere. The compost should always be kept free from weeds, as they rob it of its nutritive qualities.

The due preparation and proper consistence of the compost is of very great importance, nor will the plants succeed unless this is attended to.

Pots for blooming plants should be — diameter of top, 6½ inches, bottom, 4 inches and 7 inches deep; but smaller plants or offsets should have shallower pots of a proportionate width and depth. Bury the pots in wet earth first or immerse them in water for three or four days or a week.

Seed-raising of both auriculas and primulas: A hotbed with frames and glass lights is to be in readiness. Provide a box or boxes about 5 or 6 inches deep. Fill with the compost (described above), and gently shake or strike it against the ground till the earth settles a little; make the surface perfectly smooth and even, and sow the seed with the utmost regularity; then sift through a fine-wired sieve a little compost or decayed willow mould upon it, sufficient only just to cover the seed, and place the box in the frame, on the surface of the hotbed; the glasses must be placed over it, and so managed as to preserve a moderate and equal degree of warmth both day and night, and must be occasionally opened or raised up at the higher end to admit fresh air and to suffer the exhalations from the bed to escape, which is a *very* essential point.

This method forces every live grain of seed into vegetation in about three weeks if the warmth of the bed is properly kept up, whereas, by the usual mode of exposure to the air the greater part does not vegetate till the second year, and the weaker seeds, which are probably the most valuable, seldom vegetate at all. The earth and seed must always be kept moderately moist, but never very wet; the best method of watering is by means of a hard clothes-brush dipped into soft water which has had the chill taken off by standing in the sun — the hair side being quickly turned upwards and the hand rubbed briskly over it, will cause the water to fly off in the opposite direction in particles almost as fine as dew. A sufficient watering may be given in a few minutes.

If the surface of the box is inclined to become mossy or mouldy, it must be stirred all over very carefully with a pin, almost as deep as the thickness of a shilling; when plants appear, harden off, and put them where the sun will only strike them until nine in the morning. When about six leaves appear to a plant, take these out from the rest and transplant to other boxes filled with the compost; put about 1 inch and a half to 2 inches apart, and when they grow to touch each other, put into round small pots, where they should remain until they blow.

X

A TULIP INTERLUDE

As then the Tulip for her morning sup
Of heavenly vintage from the soil looks up.

OMAR KHAYYAM

EARLIES, Cottages, Darwins, Rembrandts, Breeders, By-blœms, and Bizarres. What an array of names, what a bewildering number of divisions! Not at all, to anyone who loves them. And from the fat old Hollander of long ago who gambled his fortune away on one bulb to the most modern flapper of to-day, who does not feel a stab of joy over their beauty, seen afresh each May?

Every gardener feels competent to talk, or plant, or write on tulips. The garden papers are full of suggested groupings in color schemes, lists of plantings with this and that annual or perennial — all a meaningless line of names at first, but fraught with interest to anyone who likes to take his gardening ready-made. It also gives hours of pleasant occupation, hunting the names and combinations — and costs — from the catalogues. For myself, I dread the bulbs lists, positively dread them, for I cannot be strong-minded enough to resist them — and then comes autumn with its should-be lazy golden days of leisure and riding, and then come also those important and insistent brown-paper bags of creatures that must be put in the ground at once. And, after all, you go about it happily enough when you think of the spring ahead. There is something so symbolic about a bulb, you feel it is a surety of your own future spring, when in October you bury it as you chant Shelly's "Ode to the West Wind" —

> "O thou
> Who chariotest to their dark wintry bed
> The wingéd seeds, where they lie cold and low,
> Each like a corpse within its grave, until
> Thine azure sister of the Spring shall blow
> Her clarion o'er the dreaming Earth."

Thus it happens, year after year, you note in May, when all your color pictures are unfolding, "There must be a more brilliant touch there against that dark shrubbery corner; how well a Sir Harold, or even the always reliable Farncombe Sanders, or that splendid Professor Rauwenhof would look!" And down goes one's pencil and the inevitable begins. Or "What is more enchanting than the graceful swaying stems of Flamingo, that delightful pink Cottager!" Once we ordered Fanny, because I was called so; she was so beautiful, one felt crushed trying to live up to her, and she has never since been purchased again.

Earlies are not much used in the garden I make, except some doubles like the orange Count von Leicester, for the plantings are for May and must not be marred by any ripening stalks. That must come later and come all at once. So we commence with the Cottages, and of these are many later ones whose time of bloom runs almost parallel with the early and middle Darwins. One soon gets to know the hour of their striking, remembering that this year's planting will be earlier than their mates who have been in several years. Note also the expected time of blooming in the catalogues by the numeral placed after the name. One needs the yellows of the Cottages, as there are none except some novelties, still expensive, in the Darwins. The Breeders give strong dark bronzes and purples and golds. The Rembrandts, Byblœms, and Bizarres one tries here and there, using their striped and feathered effects as one does the gay chintzes in sunny living rooms.

Everyone has favorites among these sections. Mine were found long ago when the Dutch lists gave funny meagre descriptions and one's imagination did the rest, always to be far more rewarded by stunning beauty than one expected. Nowadays the catalogues leave nothing to the imagination and often overdo it, so disappointment occurs and the novelties wear out one's pocketbook alarmingly. It is well to have one's favorites among the old, tried, and true, yet one succumbs to a few of the new each year.

Here are some of my tried and true: Cottage Picotee is as charming (and cheap) as one would wish. She — her synonym is so touching, Maidens Blush — lives always in one long west border. Coming up pale creamy yellow-white, the longish slender flower is edged with the tiniest frill of deep pink; this deepens and flushes down the petals day by day until within a week the border is full of dainty pink tulips where white had been before. They show well between the iris clumps then almost in bloom, old *I. florentina* and *flavescens*. Sometimes Rembrandts in feathered pinks are here, but not for long. Every four or five years more Picotees are put in, as others "fire" with that mysterious disease which they say "Semesan," the new disinfectant, will cure; or bulbs are cut and sliced by spading around some recalcitrant perennial.

In the other border of this terrace go the Breeder Cardinal Manning (syn. Goliath, Kinscourt). Again an old tried favorite, again one that is completely satisfying. Who that